333 DAYS

PERSONAL MEMOIRS FROM A REFUGEE CAMP

JACEK
LASZKIEWICZ

Order this book online at www.trafford.com
or email orders@trafford.com

Most Trafford titles are also available at major online book retailers.

Printed in the United States of America.

ISBN: 978-1-4669-4235-6 (sc)
ISBN: 978-1-4669-4237-0 (hc)
ISBN: 978-1-4669-4236-3 (e)

Library of Congress Control Number: 2012915212

Trafford rev. 11/01/2012

 www.trafford.com

North America & international
toll-free: 1 888 232 4444 (USA & Canada)
phone: 250 383 6864 ♦ fax: 812 355 4082

I am dedicating this book to both my sons, **Adrian** and **Krystian**

PREFACE

In 1985 I was 22, college educated, naive, stubborn (still am!) and a young father. My first son, Krystian, had just turned two and stayed behind in Gdańsk with his mother. I had very little life experience, spoke only Polish, and was dreaming of a better life in the West, away from communist Poland. At that time neither I nor anybody else would ever have predicted that the communist system in Eastern Europe would collapse so rapidly. It took only another four years to bring the whole of the Soviet Bloc to its knees and the biggest contributors to that fall were the President of the United States, Ronald Reagan; Gorbachev with his *perestroika*, which was widely spreading across Eastern Europe; and the leader of the Roman Catholic Church, Pope John Paul II.

Today, 27 years later, the turmoil of world events never ceases to amaze me. In the summer of '95, I left Winnipeg with my family and moved to the West Coast, settling in the city of New Westminster, the smallest of Greater Vancouver's sixteen municipalities. Long before this, however, right after the fall of the Berlin Wall and the release of the first independent version of Microsoft Windows, our second son, Adrian, was born. Today, Adrian, at the age of 23, is a graduate from the British Columbia Institute of Technology and is working as a car mechanic in Burnaby. His older brother, Krystian, graduated from Langara College in Energy Healing. Now, however, in his late twenties, he is a self employed financial planner and continues to grow as an entrepreneur.

Unfortunately, my marriage disintegrated and after 17 years Renata and I chose to go our separate ways. Ten years on, we still maintain a friendship and have a healthy respect for each others' lives.

While communism in Europe was dismantling, 46 years of *apartheid* (racial segregation) in South Africa ended, initiated by the election of F.W. de Klerk, a supporter of multi-racial democracy, and the release of Nelson Mandela from Robben Island prison. Mandela, of course, became the first black President of South Africa in 1994.

The most talked-about news of the late '90s was the *Millennium Bug*, or 'Y2K,' and the threat of computer systems crashing worldwide. Despite the widespread panic built on fear, confusion and wild speculations, we passed smoothly into the new millennium without any significant incidents. Then the *dot-com* bubble burst followed closely by the shocking 9/11 attacks on the World Trade Centre in New York. These events led to the military conflict in the Middle East, which divided us and changed the course of modern history and the way we live today.

Passport please . . .
Are you carrying any liquids, gels or sharp objects in your bag, sir?
Remove your shoes and take your belt off, please!
No, no . . . the laptop goes into another bin!

These are the stark new parametres of the realities of today's world travelling! The introduction of the Euro, the common currency among the European Union members, reshaped the European financial system. Boxing Day of 2004 became the last day for thousands – no, in fact nearly a quarter of a million-people who lost their lives in South-East Asia. This tragedy was triggered by a mega-thrust earthquake in the Indian Ocean near Indonesia, followed by the devastating force of tsunamis. The sub-prime mortgages and the Lehman Brothers' bankruptcy announcement in 2008 brought the American and the European economies to their knees, causing a global financial crisis. The campaign slogan "Change we can believe in" came in with the victory of Barack Obama, the first African-American to be elected President of the Unites States.

Three years prior to this historic election, I met Katie, my life companion and love. Barely ten months after meeting, in early August of 2006, we took our vows on top of the first peak of the Stawamus Chief Mountain in Squamish, one hour north of West Vancouver. Relatives and friends, 54 people in total, joined us for this unique wedding hike. Some traveled from Portland, Montreal, and Toronto; others traveled from as far away as England and Japan.

*   *   *

There are times in our lives when we face the challenge of making a decision that is going to change our predefined role, the role or a position that everyone expects from us to fill including our parents, friends or even the neighbours. As soon we leave the environment we are accustomed to or are expected to fit into, we encounter opposition from those we have trusted as well as the encouragement from those we would never expect it from, or perhaps those we haven't even met yet. Being a young father I observe, I listen, and then eventually I ask: "Why? Does this whole think make sense? Why am I still here?" At this time it is 1985 and I don't believe or see the light at the end of the tunnel. Instead I see a dysfunctional country dominated by corruption, lies, and oppression. The economical situation is just as bad the political are. The empty shelves in the convenience or department stores are part of reality. The shortages of the essential goods like butter, sugar, coffee, toilet paper or even soap become a struggle for the working masses. The government housing turns out to be a complete fiasco and the young family waits, on average, up to 25 years to get their own apartment. There are countless examples of the communist system failing to deliver what their leaders have promised. Some of us are not patient enough to wait endlessly for a miracle pill to treat the ill patient that is the communist system.

On March 17, 1985, I left Gdańsk on a charter flight to Rome. There were over a hundred of us, including clerical staff, and I was the youngest. After landing at Fiumicino International Airport in Rome and clearing customs, Father Tadeusz, the leader of our pilgrimage, collected our passports to lock them in a safety deposit box. This was one of the preventative measures put in place to discourage anyone from defecting. At that time, the church authorities assured Polish officials that anyone travelling to the Vatican in groups organized by the church would return back home. My plan, however, was a little different. After five days of exploring Italy, I decided to make my move. There was only one problem: My passport was still locked in the safe. However, by using my imagination and creativity, I managed to convince one of the Roman Catholic nuns to give me back my passport. Consequently, I was able to separate from the rest of the group as I had planned. Months later, this decision caused a few headaches for those in charge of our group and especially for that one unforgettable nun. Who knows what path my life would have taken had it not been for her?

At first, Rome was overwhelming. I found this ancient city dirty, noisy and chaotic. At that point, though, it didn't really matter as I was on my way to the Termini train station, my destination Latina, a city located 60 km south of Rome. This is where my journey begins.

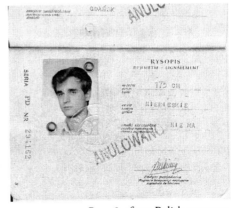

Page 3 of my Polish passport.

March 22, 1985 - Friday

The refugee camp or, in Italian, *campo*, is located on the premises of a decommissioned military base. There are a number of barracks and one main building known as Building B, which is mainly occupied by families and married couples. The camp's capacity is around 900 refugees who are mainly from Eastern European countries such as Yugoslavia, Czechoslovakia, Albania, Romania, Bulgaria, the Soviet Union and Hungary; the largest group of refugees is from Poland.

At 4:20 p.m., I enter the gate of the camp. After surrendering my Polish passport to the Italian authorities, I am directed to a so-called 'transit area,' an area where all the newcomers spend the first few days after arrival. During this time, I meet four other Poles: Jurek Majewski, Wojtek Kowalczyk, Mirek Kostrzyński from Warsaw, and the fourth, Wiesiek Kowalski, from Wrocław. All four met and travelled on the same tour organized by Warszawski Sport-Tourist, which some ironically called the 'Polish Immigration Agency.' For many Poles this was their only chance – and the only legal way – to get out of communist Poland. I am the youngest at 22 years old. Jurek, a vet by trade, is 32 and the eldest. He speaks some English and apparently his father or uncle lives in Montreal, Canada. My first night is on a bunk bed.

March 23rd - Saturday

Since early morning, I have been taking care of the legal formalities related to my arrival at the camp. After an interview with local authorities and the Italian police, I receive a formal identification document, which replaces my Polish passport while I am in Italy. From now on, I am number 11283. Next is the visit to the warehouse where I pick up supplies: a single bed, detergent, two sheets and some blankets, five BIC razors, a bar of soap, toilet paper, dishwashing liquid, toothpaste, cutlery and two plastic plates. Shortly afterwards, I move to barrack H, room 43, which sleeps eight people. The room is filthy with a cold cement floor, dirty windows and rusty steel cabinets. Five Poles

My new ID.

occupy the room: the eldest is 43 year old Jurek, also known as 'Nero,' as well as Przemyk, Romek, Lucek (the coal miner from Silesia), and the fifth, me. The state of the room tells me that they don't really care about how we live. In fact, a large part of their daily activity involves drinking booze. I guess I'm not so lucky with my room assignment.

Barrack H is no better, with its cement floors; common bathrooms with no windows; a hot water supply that lasts on average two hours a day; and restroom cabins that are long-drops with no doors. Hmmm . . . interesting.

My new home.

March 25th - Monday

Today, 'Nero' has accepted two newcomers into our room: Leszek Piłaszewicz and Heniek Lacheta are brothers-in-law, both from Białystok, Poland. Leszek left behind his wife, Lucyna, and their eight-year old son. Heniek is a bachelor. With these latest additions, the room is full. It doesn't take me long to work out that the main reason for 'Nero' accepting newcomers, including me, is driven by money. Every new face comes with a fat wallet and is expected to sponsor a 'welcome party.' 'Nero' and Lucek must be very disappointed to find out that I am not willing to blow my US $160 on alcohol.

Early afternoon, 11 Poles, including a small child, checked in at the gate. All came via Sweden. To prevent extradition to communist Poland, the whole group hired a mini-van driver (for 2,500 Swedish Kronas per person) to get them safely across Europe to Italy. The extraordinary part of this trip was that only the driver had the required visas to cross all border checkpoints. Before reaching the border, the driver stopped the van and let out all the passengers. They then had to cross the border on foot a distance away from the crossing and meet the driver on the other side to continue the journey. This procedure was repeated five times.

March 27th - Wednesday

Until the age of 11, I spent lengthy periods of time in different hospitals where I was treated for asthma. In fact, I completed the first grade of elementary school in the Rabka Rehabilitation Centre in southern Poland. The hospital was crammed full with both children and teenagers, all with their own heartbreaking illness. It was so hard to watch a young soul coughing and gasping for air. I remember spending long days and nights sitting in a hospital bed and silently crying for help, which never came. Overcoming asthma was my passport to a better life: active participation in sport and then competitive judo helped with that.

Today, I passed my medical, which consisted of an Italian doctor asking questions and recording the answers. "Did you or do you have asthma?" I was asked. "No," I answer with confidence. Immigration is at stake and I am not willing to reveal my medical past.

It has been ten days since I left Gdańsk. Yesterday was the first time I spoke with Renata, my wife, and my two-year old son, Krystian. This past February 14th was his birthday. The local post office, (SIP

Communication Centre) provides an international telephone service. The procedure is fairly simple: pay, register and wait. A clerk behind the counter calls your name and points to an available booth as soon as the telephone connection has been established. Typically it takes between ten to 20 minutes to secure a connection.

Krystian is full of energy, and raising him is physically very demanding. Even though Renata can count on the help of our families, day-to-day responsibilities come with a huge sacrifice, dedication and patience. Now, my parenting role has been limited to writing letters only.

March 28th - Thursday

I have been in Rome since early morning. I came here with Artur Nieszczerzewicz, one of the 11 refugees who arrived a few days ago from Sweden. At 10 a.m. we walk to the Swedish Consulate. Artur wants to find out if he has any chance of immigrating back to Sweden, where he and his mom spent nine months before arriving in Latina. A consulate clerk notifies him that his chance of being accepted by the Swedish government is very slim and he should consider another option. It looks like Canada after all.

Meals are served in a common building and always at a designated time. We have a two-hour window to pick up each meal. If you miss this window, you have to wait until the next meal. This evening, I ran into Adam Domżalski on the way to the kitchen.

"Oh my God, what are you doing here?" I ask.
"And what are you doing here?" Adam asks with a grin.

"We came here a month ago on February 13th," he adds. "Listen, why don't you come over when you finish supper? We are in building B, room 17. Małgosia will be really surprised to see you."

Right after supper, I give Małgosia a hug. Both of us can't believe that we are meeting here, in the refugee camp. Małgosia and I graduated from the same elementary school in Gdańsk. We have a few friends in common and many shared memories. "What a small world!" I think and smirk to myself. They are on track to immigrate to California where Adam has relatives. We spend the rest of the evening catching up.

March 31st - Sunday

"Bless me, Father, for I have sinned. It has been a year since my last confession." The 'Sacrament of Penance' or simply 'confession' is offered on camp premises in a building that serves as a sanctuary, every Saturday and Sunday. The masses are in Polish and aside from the spiritual enrichment, they are a good opportunity to meet other immigrants.

Latina 31.03.1985

Hi!

Dad, I am not sure how you reacted, or will react to my decision to not come back to Poland. I just wanted you to know that, whatever your reaction, my decision was not made overnight. Both Renata and I have been planning for this over the last few months and put a lot of thought into it. Please take a look at what's really happening in Poland today. The housing situation is in dire straits and housing is no longer accessible to the average citizen. The 'townhome' project in Gdansk, which we signed in for, has become financially not feasible.

At the moment I am in a refugee camp in the small city of Latina, located 62 kilometres south of Rome. There are nearly a thousand of us here, the majority of whom are Poles, and the others are Albanians, Czechs, Romanians, Bulgarians and other nationalities. The camp conditions are bad (concrete floors, rusty steel cabinets, filthy walls and leaking window frames). The bathrooms and toilets are the worst though.

The food is okay, but barely enough. In a nutshell, nobody will die of hunger here, nor will anyone gain weight. Since I have decided to immigrate to Canada I will be spending a year living in these conditions, as that's how long the immigration process to Canada takes.

There are many reasons why I picked Canada for my new home; one of the main reasons is that the Canadian Government will sponsor me without the requirement of political asylum, unlike the United States, which requires you to find a sponsor and your decision to immigrate has to be politically motivated.

I'm quite sure you'll be interested to know that none of us get any pocket money here which is quite tough on smokers (their own supplies end quickly). The camp authorities supply us with sanitary needs such as detergent, soap, shaving supplies and toilet paper. There is also a Polish School for children here and opportunities to study English.

It is also possible to work in the camp, but compensation is minimal and ranges from L5,000 to L 8,000 (US $2.5-4) per day. A more effective way to make money is to find work outside of the camp and if you're lucky you can make between L20,000-25,000, which is more than US$10 for an eight-hour work day. I've only been here for ten days and haven't got around to finding work yet. There is a church on the premises of the camp. The catholic services are each Saturday at 4 p.m., and each Sunday at 9:30 a.m. Today I went to Confession. I hope this short overview of the camp was educational for you and objective.

Considering all the challenges I have no doubt that I will succeed here and for now that is the most important thing for me.

Now I wish you all a Happy Easter, 'Buona Pasqua'. Of course, please forward my best wishes to Grandma as well.

My address as follows: J.L.
                                                 Via XXIV Maggio 3
                                                 04-100 Latina
                                                 Wlochy (Italy)

April 2nd - Tuesday

Today, I went to the market – which is two kilometres from the city centre – with Wojtek K., (whom I met in the transit area). The market is considerably larger than the one I used to go to in Gdańsk, known as *Rynek*. Even though I am on a tight budget, I went on a shopping spree: a new grey tracksuit, two t-shirts (blue and red), and a pair of flip-flops. In total: L32,000[1]. Not bad, considering I am dressed from head to toe. Wojtek ends up with one grey shirt.

Street vendor
at the local market.

April 4th - Thursday

A few days ago, I started English classes for beginners. The classes are held in building B and there are 40 students in our group. Barnaba, the teacher, is from the UK. He is in his late 20s or early 30s, has a good sense of humour, wears glasses and has a thick beard. As well as English classes, Polish kids can also attend an improvised Polish elementary school. The curriculum consists of a few subjects such as Polish language, math, history, physics and even biology. Success in each subject depends on teacher availability. With no incentives on the table the school faces a continuous lack of teachers. They are not paid for their dedication, their time or their hard work. Perhaps Zachorski's organization, with its office in Rome, should take a closer look at it. Zachorski is one of four organizations that help refugees in the immigration process. To be honest, neither Adam nor I believe that Zachorski is ready to open its wallet.

---

[1]   US $1 = 2,100 lire

April 6th - Saturday

Tomorrow is Easter! Today, Małgosia, Adam and I did some Easter shopping. It took us less than 30 minutes. It's hard to believe that Easter preparations in Poland can take a week or more. This evening is clean-up time in B-17. Here I will spend my first holiday far away from home, a strange feeling indeed.

April 7th - EASTER SUNDAY

The day starts with a church service. Shortly afterwards, the three of us are back in the room ready to start the Easter feast. Małgosia does a fantastic job decorating the table. There is a basket full of dyed eggs in Italian, American, Canadian and even Polish national colours. The coloured eggs, also known as *Pisanki*, are symbolic of the Polish Easter tradition.

Easter Eggs, also known as 'Pisanki.'

In the past, only women decorated eggs. Men were not allowed to come inside the house during the process, as it was believed that they could put a spell on the eggs, and cause bad luck. Until the 12th century, the Catholic Church forbade the consumption of eggs during Easter. The church wished to distance itself from the pagan roots of the tradition connected with the cult of the dead, in which the egg played an important role as a symbol of rebirth. This ban was lifted, but it was necessary to offer a special prayer before eating. Today pisanki are hallowed on Easter Saturday, along with the traditional Easter basket. On Easter Sunday, before the ceremonial breakfast, these eggs are exchanged and shared among the family at the table.

Later on, we go for a walk to the local park. As we expect, the tennis courts are empty. On any other day all four courts would be busy. At night we talk about our relatives and friends back in Gdańsk. It's an intense and emotional time for all of us. Adam wraps up the evening with a richly patriotic repertoire of Jacek Kaczmarski's music, by many considered the voice of the anti-communist Solidarity movement in Poland. The dynamic sound of the guitar fills the walls of B-17. This intensifies our patriotism and makes us even more homesick.

April 9ᵗʰ - Tuesday

Exactly at 11 a.m., I step into the C.I.M. office, room 13. Since I decided to immigrate to Canada I am here to submit all the required paperwork. The World Council of Churches (W.C.C.) will take care of my passport formalities and any costs associated with my trip. There are a few other organizations: I.R.C.; P.A.I.R.C., also known as 'Zachorski' (with a poor reputation); U.C.E.I. (a church organization); and the Russian 'Tolstoy,' which has the best reputation and an office in Rome. Today the C.I.M. confirmed that the immigration process to Canada is quite lengthy and it can take up to 12 long months. However, my earlier decision is rock solid: I'm going to wait for Canada.

April 13ᵗʰ - Saturday

Yesterday night Adam took a train north to Milan to meet with Małgosia's brother-in-law, Mariusz, with plans to be back in Latina on Monday afternoon. The Gdańsk University of Technology (Politechnika Gdańska) appointed Mariusz to participate in some sort of science conference. This will be a great opportunity for both of them to exchange first-hand news on relatives in Poland and daily living in the camp. Meanwhile, Małgosia and I take advantage of the good weather and go to a small town called Norma, located about 14 km northeast of Latina, with a population of 3,851 and an area of 30.8 km². Mariola and Andrzej, newcomers from Gdynia in Poland, join us.

Day trip to Norma.

The city, or rather town, of Norma stands out from the mountain, 400 metres above sea level. The narrow winding streets, the cold stone buildings and the hidden street corners reflect the history of this small community, established early in the 1900s. In contrast, modern villas dominate the new section of town, which lacks the charisma of its older sister. The residential buildings perched on top of the 60-metre cliffs are both striking and memorable. It is impressive to a young chap like me. "How on earth did they build this?" I ask myself. On the way back we take a local bus and I sit with my head leaning against the window, trying to absorb as much scenery as I can. After the long 14 km hike to this small, captivating town, I am exhausted and doze off.

April 16th - Tuesday

Since yesterday, I have been sharing a new room with Leszek and Heniek. The room sleeps three and it seems to have been previously occupied by Czechoslovakian refugees, as Slovak books and magazines have been left behind. The new room is way better than the old one: the walls are fairly clean, the window has an aluminum frame and there's an improvised clothing rack. The two existing chairs are in mint condition plus the steel cabinets are also in reasonable shape. Finally, we have our own place and from now on

In a local park with Marian (C) and Leszek (R).

the room belongs to the 'Canadian gang.' All three of us signed up for Canada.

April 20ᵗʰ - Saturday

In the past three days, I received two packages from home. The first contained stationery, the second includes a book, 'Open University English,' sent by Tycjan, my best and only buddy from Gdańsk. Inside, I find a note from Renata:

> *"Kochany Jacku, przyznam się*
> *Tobie, że nawet się Cieszę z Twojego*
> *wyboru. Trzymam kciuki. Myślę*
> *o Tobie Mój Ty Kochany Biedaczku.*
> *Nie martw się, jestem ciągle myślami*
> *przy Tobie – Kochanie. Dzień po Twoim*
> *Wyjeździe przyszedł list od Magdy –*
> *Napisałem Jej gdzie jesteś. Kochanie*
> *Masz serdeczne pozdrowienia od*
> *Tycjana. Z Kamilą się jeszcze nie*
> *widziałam. Jacusiu Kocham Cię*
> *i niech Bóg ma Ciebię w swojej*
> *opiece. Całuję bardzo gorąco."*
> *Renata K.C.*

My love, I really want to thank you for these words, which I will keep close to my heart.

My friendship with Tycjan goes way back to the early seventies when both our families moved and met in the newly developed neighbourhood on Pomorska Street in Gdańsk Oliwa. Tycjan, his beautiful sister, Joanna, and his parents took possession of an apartment on the fifth floor while my mom and I moved to the seventh. Both of us enrolled in the same elementary school on Chłopska Street, less than two kilometres from where we lived. Even though the majority of our school years were spent in different classrooms in elementary school and at different post-secondary schools, our friendship never weakened and in fact has grown even stronger over the years. We both joined ZHP (the Polish Scouting and Guiding Association). This was, however, a short-lived passion for both of us but with life-long, lasting memories. We spent our free time playing tennis, kicking a ball, taking free rides on public transport to nearby Jelitkowo beach, and skipping catechism classes to dig for amber in the local sand dunes. Eventually we joined judo at the Academy of Physical Education in Gdańsk. Of course the mid-to-late teens came with house parties, nightclubs or student clubs, where we listened to Western-style live music, often the Blues. We had our first beer and cigarette together, even though neither of us really smoked. In the latter years, like many other young guys, we got involved in the political situation of communist Poland. We attended illegal lectures organized by the local churches, and participated in anti-government demonstrations and street riots. Despite the fact that we grew up in a totalitarian system and saw our parents' day-to-day struggle, life on Pomorska Street was not bad at all. We had a roof above our heads, full stomachs, and plenty of activities to keep us busy. Now, for the last five weeks, our friendship has taken different paths: I am in Latina while Tycjan is still in Gdańsk.

April 23rd - Tuesday

Laundry time.

A month ago yesterday, I arrived at the camp. I can honestly say that I am now acclimatized to this new reality, and my new way of living. Also, all the required paperwork for the immigration process to Canada has been completed. Now I just have to be patient and wait for my first interview, as it can take up to six long months to get an appointment with the Canadian Consul. This period of time will test my patience and my belief system.

I remember that it was late afternoon, the third or fourth day of our pilgrimage in March. After a long day of touring the city I came back to our temporary residence in the suburbs of Rome. As soon as I opened the door of my room I noticed a stranger, who seemed to be in his 30s, sharing the table with one of my older roommates. After a quick introduction I found out that he arrived from a refugee camp in Latina, located 60 km south of Rome and was visiting to pick up letters from his wife in Poland. This was the very first time I had heard of Latina, and I followed the stranger after he left our room to find out how to get there.

"How do I get there? What are the procedures for checking in at the camp?" I asked him.

"You need to get to Termini station in central Rome and buy a ticket to Latina which will cost L3,000," he replied. He added, "The train ride takes around one hour, then you need to take a local bus for a few minutes. When you enter the camp gates, you will need to give up your passport to one of the guards. There are many Poles in the camp." I thanked him and we shook hands.

April 26th - Friday

Finally mail! Today I got four letters and an Easter greeting card from my Mom. Two letters are from Renata, and one from my friend, Magda. I met Magda at Mazury (the Masuria Lake District) located in the northeastern region of Poland. Mazury is famous for its beautiful landscape and 2,000 lakes, a paradise for water sports and recreational activities. Magda, who is more or less my age, is a beautiful brunette with long hair that reaches past her shoulders, striking hazel eyes, and dark skin, unusual for someone with a Polish background. Although we never dated I was always attracted to Magda.

Besides offering a serene and beautiful landscape, Mazury played a significant role in the Second World War. Between the summer of 1941 and the autumn of 1944, Adolf Hitler spent 800 days in the steel-reinforced concrete bunkers of his Eastern Front military headquarters at Wilczy Szaniec, or the 'Wolf's Lair.' It was here, on July 20, 1944, that Colonel Claus von Stauffenberg led a coup and a failed assassination attempt against Hitler. This consequently led to his and the conspirators' arrests, and executions by firing squad the following day.

The last letter was from cousin Marek who lives in Germany. Marek's letter was unpleasant and very cold.

"Dziekuję Ci za list, ale naprawdę nie wiem czy dobrze zrobiłeś, mimo 4 lat, które tu jesteśmy nie idzie nam dobrze jak żeśmy sobie wyobrażali ..."
"Zwarzywszy że masz żonę i dziecko twoja decyzja o emigracji jest dla mnie niezrozumiała i nieodpowiedzialną."

"Thank you for your letter. However, I am not sure if you made a good decision. We have been here (in Germany) for four years and we are still struggling ..."
"Knowing that you're married with a child, your decision to immigrate is irresponsible and not justified."

Marek has been away from the realities of day-to-day living in socialist Poland for four years, and this has skewed his perception on what's really happening there.

April 28th - Sunday

Praying for work.

Every morning, between 20 and 30 *stranieros* (foreigners) line up on Via XXIV Maggio 3. We stand or sit on the street curb patiently waiting for a car to stop, but only a few of us will be selected to work today. The majority will find a job for two or three days and only a few will find work for a week or more. Even though it is illegal for refugees to work, this routine repeats itself every single morning. The local authorities and the camp personnel are indifferent and simply close their eyes to it. Yesterday was my turn, my first day of work on Italian soil. Andrzej Godlewski and I started work at 7 a.m. We were supposed to finish at around 4 p.m. but instead we got back to camp at 7:30 p.m. My day started with a shovel in my hand, mixing sand and cement. It took less than 30 minutes for the first blisters to appear; one after the other, they started to pop while my hands chafed against the shovel's wooden handle. Meanwhile, Andrzej was digging a hole with a pickaxe, working on the foundations for a new building. I joined him later on, but I was mainly digging holes for grapevines. At the beginning I coped fairly well, but as the hours passed my energy level dropped dramatically. The heat, lack of breaks, and effort of digging through challenging dry and wet clay exhausted us. We worked three hours longer than expected, but we were not paid extra. I tried to challenge our employer, but Andrzej didn't back me up and I accomplished nothing. We each ended up with L25,000 in our pockets, and I found out that I wouldn't be needed the next day.

April 30th - Tuesday

Of all the ethnic groups, the Albanians seem to be the most united, but also the least trusted by others. They are known for theft around the camp and, on occasion, for bullying other refugees. Most of them speak fluent Italian, which works to their advantage when looking for work.

The most visible figure in the camp is 'yogi', a monster from Romania. This gigantic, walking sculpture of muscles captures everyone's attention. For some, 'yogi' represents a symbol of strength and power; to others, fear and intimidation. Even the owners of the popular nightclub 'Felix' recognized his strength and hired him as a bouncer. In the kitchen where we pick up our meals, it is comical to watch him. His massive, oversized hands struggle to carry the plates, piled high with food. "Will he drop it or not?" I ask myself. After all, muscles are not the answer to everything. A few of us silently chuckle as we watch 'yogi' leave the kitchen.

May 1st - Wednesday

May Day, or International Worker's Day, celebrates the social and economic achievements of the labour movement. The idea of a 'worker's holiday' began in Australia. It was back in 1856 when the Stonemasons' Society, in what was then the colony of Victoria (now the State of Victoria), led the march for the 'Eight Hour Day,' the most dramatic achievement of the early Trade Union Movement. A memorial statue etched with the numbers 888 – representing eight hours of work, eight hours of recreation, and eight hours of rest – sits on the corner of Lygon Street and Victoria Parade in Melbourne to this day.

The May Day celebrations have always been a great opportunity for the communist governments to reinforce their socialistic ideologies and underline how much stronger they are compared with the corrupt and money-driven greed of a capitalistic society. Conscious or subconscious participation in these staged and well-organized parades is used to the fullest potential by the propaganda media machines. In the last few years (1981-84), as the fall of communism approached, the dynamics of the parades changed into spontaneous street demonstrations against the regime. No longer are there banners with slogans supporting the communist party: instead the banners say 'out with communism' or 'let's use the baton on the general's ass' (General Jaruzelski is currently in power). As expected, the response is usually motorized civic militia force, also known as ZOMO, equipped with batons, shields, water cannons, military vehicles and even tanks. Are the events of the last four years going to be repeated? Will this so-called 'dialogue' between Jaruzelski's regime and the banned Solidarity Union continue? I think so. In fact, I'm sure there will be anti-government demonstrations on the streets of Polish cities today. The big question is, which cities will participate?

May 4th - Saturday

Finally, I received some information on May Day demonstrations in Poland. According to the correspondents of *Voice of America*, the demonstrations and riots were the most violent of the last four years.

Fifteen thousand demonstrators took to the streets of Warsaw and more than 2,000 in Gdańsk. In the country's capital, a large number of protestors were arrested, including the democratic leader of the opposition, Jacek Kuroń. In Gdańsk, some people were wounded in the clash with the ZOMO. The anti-government demonstrations also took place in Nowa Huta, Wrocław, and Poznań. Once again the nation demonstrated its opposition to Jaruzelski's regime.

The Voice of America was organized and began broadcasting in February of 1942 under the Office of War Information, with news programs aimed at areas under occupation of Nazi Germany. The initial announcement of the VOA stated, "Daily at this time, we shall speak to you about America and the war. The news may be good or bad. We shall tell you the truth." Today VOA broadcasts approximately 1,500 hours of news, information, educational, and cultural programming every week to an estimated worldwide audience of 134 million people. Next to Radio Free Europe, it is the only source of any reliable information to listeners of Eastern European countries, ranging from industrial workers to dissident leaders.

May 5th - Sunday

This afternoon, Adam and I decided to play tennis on the local courts, located in the school grounds. Out of school hours, the courts are always empty. Adam owns a couple of old wooden tennis racquets and three Slazenger tennis balls. For my first match in five years, I am wearing jeans and a t-shirt. It's not hard to imagine how the game ended – I lack a good serve and backhand stroke, and my forehand and drop shots are useless. Even though my lob is strong, the final score is 3-0 for Adam. I threaten him with revenge.

Tennis in Poland took off in the late '70s and early '80s with the great international success of Wojtek Fibak, back then the star of Polish tennis and one of the best doubles players in the world. Later on, he became a prominent businessman and art collector, living between Poland and Monaco. I remember in my teens hitting the ball first with my wooden, and then aluminum, framed racquets. What we lacked in equipment we made up in competitiveness. We could spend hours on the blacktop playing singles or doubles in self-proclaimed tournaments, or watching the Davis Cup or Wimbledon on the television. Later that day we would pretend to be Bjorn Borg, Ilie Nastase, Tom Okker or the short-tempered John McEnroe.

May 6th - Monday

Today is a big day! Andrzej, Mariola and her son, Artur, are leaving the camp. This is the day they have been waiting for since Easter: They're getting transferred to the Barba Hotel in the suburbs of Rome. Even though we are surprised by the news, we are all happy for them and a little envious. The camp's filth, odour, and dampness will be replaced with clean rooms, showers and reasonably good meals. Of course Andrzej will be the happiest to leave, as he complained continuously about the quality of food here. My problem is the quantity rather than the quality, but that's another story. Young Artur looks pretty happy, too. After all, no more school for him. None of the facilities outside of the camp have resources to provide any classes. Unfortunately most of the parents overlook this important responsibility and their children will miss out on a year of schooling. The bus with the 30 other refugees left around 10:30 a.m.

It was a warm late afternoon. They were in the same room, one sitting at the table, the other standing. The guy who is standing holds in his right hand a sharp knife, or rather an envelope opener in the shape of a medieval knight's sword. The guy sitting is within easy reaching distance of a loaded gun. He knows that any sudden move can cost him his life, or at the very least, severe injury. The guy standing watches the suspect slowly reaching for the gun. "Don't do it, or I will throw the 'knife,'" he says. In a split second the other guy grabs the gun, but just a fraction of a second before pulling the trigger he falls to the floor with the 'knife' hanging from his kneecap. "Son of a bitch," Tycjan screams with his face contorted in sheer terror and pain. "Jacek, why the hell did you do that?" he shrieked. Still writhing in pain he added, "This was only supposed to be a game." "Tycjan, I warned you not to do it," I calmly replied and then I burst out laughing.

May 7th - Tuesday

Last Saturday, I received letters from Mom and Renata. The second letter is a reply to mine, which I sent over a month ago.

My love, I admire your strength and dedication in raising our son, Krystian. I can only imagine how difficult and challenging it is for you. Today, and forever, my heart and my spirit are with you. The numerous letters and telephone calls bring us closer but the most important thing is the faith that we have in each other and in the decision we made.

On Saturday, Adam and I did some major furniture shopping. After an extensive search we came back to camp with two 'armchairs' and a 'sofa.' All the pieces of furniture come from a dumpster and most likely used to be part of a FIAT 127. Before celebrating the 'purchase' we needed to modify an existing table so it could match the new furniture. After a few minutes of 'engineering debate,' we flipped the table upside down and broke off all four legs. Now we have an official entertainment corner, also called the 'Japanese corner,' with a low seating arrangement.

May 11th - Saturday

And here I am, no longer part of a six-person gang, now left on my own. At noon Małgosia and Adam left for the Barba Hotel in Rome, the very same hotel Andrew and Mariola were transferred to. Last night the three of us got together for a farewell party. Adam played some music on his guitar, mainly songs from the *First Independent Songs Festival* in Gdańsk. The lyrics of Jacek Kaczmarski's songs are patriotic and raise our spirits. We were enjoying the music and a bottle of *Peroni* (local beer) and didn't even notice that it was 1 a.m., time for me to leave B-17.

This evening I went to the cinema to watch *Yentl* with American star, Barbra Streisand. Even though the film was dubbed in Italian I still enjoyed it. Every Thursday the camp authorities distribute free movie tickets to the refugees. Perhaps they are trying to compensate for the camp conditions we have to put up with.

May 12th - Sunday

On this day in 1935, the great Polish revolutionary and statesman, First Chief of State Marshall Piłsudski, died. This revered general did more than any other single Pole, working primarily with Poles and on Polish soil to achieve the independence of Poland after the First World War. During his funeral President Mościcki eulogized the Marshall:

"He was the king of our hearts and the sovereign of our will. During a half-century of his life's travails, he captured heart after heart, soul after soul, until he had drawn the whole of Poland within the purple of his royal spirit . . . He gave Poland freedom, boundaries, power and respect."

Shamefully, today the history books barely mention the name of Józef Piłsudski and if they do, his image has been maligned by communist propaganda attacks. Some collegiate teachers even compare Pilsudski's dictatorship traits with fascism. Luckily, there are many independent publications where we can learn the truth about this great patriot and national hero; sadly, there is no special celebration in camp today.

This afternoon, Leszek came to visit Latina. He now lives in Rome where he found work. Before catching the morning train, Leszek went to a Polish church near Venice Square in Rome and along with a few hundred other immigrants, he participated in a Sunday mass fully dedicated to Marshall Piłsudski. Too bad I couldn't be there.

May 13th - Monday

As planned, Jurek and I go for a day trip to Rome. I have to take care of some paperwork to allow Renata and Krystian to travel abroad. An Italian notary public, Ms. Elvira Belleli, has approved the authenticity of the documents, which cost L5,000. On the way back to the Termini train station, I mail the documents to Gdańsk. The only other thing left to take care of is a letter of invitation for both of them so they can get permission to leave Poland. The whole idea is for the three of us to be re-united in Italy so that we can immigrate to Canada together. Later on, this plan changes and Renata and Krystian will remain in Poland.

JACEK LASZKIEWICZ
Ul. Pomorska 94A/64
80-333 GDANSK

U P O W A Z N I E N I E

Ja Jacek Laszkiewicz urodzony 05.01.1963 roku w Gdansku zamieszkaly w Gdansku ulica Pomorska 94A/64 posiadajacy paszport serii PD numer 294162 wydany przez WUSW w Gdansku, waznosc paszportu mija w miesiacu styczniu 1987r. wyrazam zgode mojej zonie Renacie Laszkiewicz corce Ryszarda z domu Niedzwie- dzaka urodzonej 02.06.1963 roku w Gdansku zamieszkalej w Gdansku ulica Pomor- ska 94A/64 na wszelkie wyjazdy zagraniczne wraz z synem.
Krystian Laszkiewicz urodzony 14.02.1983 roku w Gdansku.

Oboje z zona sprawujemy nad dzieckiem pelna wladze rodzicielska.

Dott. ELVIRA BELLELLI
NOTAIO IN ROMA
Via Prisco Attanci, 21
ROMA - Tel. 42 41.515

AUTENTICA DI FIRMA
REPUBBLICA ITALIANA

Io sottoscritto dottor Elvira BELLELLI Notaio in Roma, iscritto nel ruolo dei Distretti Notarili Riuniti di Roma, Velletri e Ci- vitavecchia,dichiaro e certifico che il signor
JACEK LASZKIEWICZ nato in Gdansk (Polonia) il 5 gennaio 1963, della cui identità personale mi sono accertata a mezzo Passapor- to polacco serie PD NR 294162,ha firmato l'atto che precede in mia presenza,previa sua espressa rinuncia con il mio censenso al- l'assistenza dei testi.$
Roma, tredici maggio Millenovecentoottantacinque.

May 15th - Wednesday

I had to wait for four hours at the police station before I was called in. Then, in less than 15 minutes, the *verbale* or, in other words, the police questioning, is over and I was on my way back to camp. From now on I am on record with the local police department. The *verbale* however, goes beyond the criminal record check. Standing next to the police officer was a CIA agent whose role was to verify the accuracy of the information collected by the CIA field agents while spying in Eastern Europe. This mainly applies to military bases, the size of the military units, and the military rank each of us held before arriving in Latina. The CIA is also interested in infrastructure such as the bridges and power stations.

May 18th - Saturday

For the last two days, Leszek has been working on a construction site. So far he has been paid L80,000, which is very good pay. However, we realize, from checking his hands that his work is physically very demanding and that's one of the reasons he's paid so well.

May 21st - Tuesday

The last couple of evenings we spent watching professional boxing in front of the black and white TV. Even though the fights are televised with a few days' delay, it doesn't matter to us and we consider it a treat to watch the pros. This brings back memories of my grandma Valeria passionately staring at the boxing fights with a cigarette in one hand and a cup of black coffee in the other.

On the first night we watched the fight between Puerto Rican Wilfredo 'Bazooka' Gómez and American, Rocky Lockridge. After a close 15-round bout, Gómez won by a unanimous decision, winning the WBA Super Featherweight title. The second night of boxing was a long-awaited fight between the heavyweight champion Larry Holmes and contender Carl 'Truth' Williams. After 15 rounds, Holmes retained the IBF title. Not everyone agrees with the verdict of the three judges in Reno, Nevada.

May 23rd - Thursday

Watering melons at the local farm.

About time . . . I finally got work! It has been two months since I arrived at the camp and this is the first time I have found work. Henry and two Albanians also managed to get work. In the first couple of days the working conditions are outstanding – we have a one-hour long siesta break, with sandwiches, plus wine and water for lunch. Prior to returning to work, each of us has a shot of espresso. This brings us back to life and we are ready for an excruciatingly hot afternoon planting melons, with temperatures reaching 35C plus. At 5 p.m., we are all paid L30,000 and arrive back at the camp, happy. Tomorrow, *lavoro* again . . .

May 25th - Saturday

There must be more than ten greenhouses where the four of us are picking strawberries. In addition, Signore Vastola owns a huge melon plantation, which is located a few kilometres away from his house. I am quite sure he's doing well financially.

The last couple of days, we were removing infected zucchini plants from the greenhouses. The temperature inside reached 45C: It was hot, dry and dusty. The infected plants ended up on a tractor-trailer, and Mario, the owner's son, disposed of them. After a few hours of working in these conditions, my allergies and asthma started to affect my breathing and I felt sick. Both Antonio and Mario noticed that I was struggling, so they told me to sit and rest. I spent the remainder of the morning recovering in the shade of a tree. "That's it for me and a well-paid job," I think to myself.

Punctually at noon we take a break, or in other words, it's *siesta time.* Today's lunch was delicious and served at the Vastolas' home. Signora Vastola prepared the cabbage rolls and fantastic pasta with green beans. The second dish consisted of chips, sardines and, in keeping with tradition, plenty of wine and water. Today I am more cautious with drinking wine as yesterday I had one glass too many and was light-headed. Luckily the shot of espresso saved me from embarrassment. Don't be mistaken: No good lunch is complete without dessert, and today is no exception. We had homegrown fresh strawberries. "Oh gosh! So sweet, so good . . ."

May 28th - Tuesday

The sixth day of work for Signore Vastola.

Today is my sixth day of work. Even though the work is physically undemanding, it is still strenuous due to the heat and the complete lack of a breeze. I took my 35mm Soviet-made camera to take pictures on the job. Zenit is one of the most popular SLR cameras in the Eastern Bloc countries. It is widely available, simple to use, and most importantly an affordable option compared with its East German 35mm rival, Praktica, which is more technically advanced. Brands like Nikon, Minolta or Cannon are the ultimate dream of every photographer in Poland, but only a small percentage of the photographic elite can afford such a luxury; others will have to satisfy their appetites by reading colourful magazines or brochures. This is the reality of living under a communist regime.

We finished work punctually at 5 p.m. and Antonio drove us back to camp. His younger brother, Mario, studies at night. Signore Vastola also has a daughter, but I still haven't met her. Tomorrow is another day of work and then in the evening, the UEFA Champions League final between Liverpool and Juventus. This should be a very exciting game between these English and Italian football giants. My heart is with Juve and their two star players, French Michel Platini and a Polish striker 'Zibi' Boniek, wearing black and white striped shirt.

May 29th - Wednesday

Thirty-eight dead and more than 200 injured. What a tragedy! This is the unconfirmed number of casualties of today's UEFA Champions League final. An hour and half before the scheduled kick-off, a large group of English Liverpool fans breached a fence separating them from rival Italian Juventus fans. The Juventus fans retreated from them into a concrete retaining wall. Many Italian fans seated near the wall were crushed and died, or were badly injured, and eventually the wall collapsed.

The game officials decided that the match should go ahead to prevent further violence. The only goal of the game came from a penalty kick in the 56th minute as 'Zibi' was brought down by Gary Gillespie. Michele Platini did not waste the opportunity and scored the only goal of the match. Juventus FC won 1-0 and won the European Cup for the first time ever.

Witnessing this pre-match drama on TV was shocking and disturbing. Nobody could ever have anticipated such a tragic outcome of tonight's final. We're speechless and ask ourselves, "Who is to blame? The English soccer hooligans or perhaps the stadium security personnel? What about the hesitant police officers?" No matter where the responsibility lies, this will not bring back those who lost their lives.

May 31st - Friday

Oh my, this was the ninth day of *lavoro*. We are still getting paid the same wage, which is L30,000 each. Yesterday Leszek left the camp and was transferred to Rome, to a hotel known as the 'Sporting Residence.' Wiesiek 'Aussie' Kowalski (who applied to immigrate to Australia) moved into our room from the room next door, taking Leszek's spot. Wiesiek is from Wrocław in southern Poland, and his wife and months-old child are in Poland.

June 2nd - Sunday

Happy Birthday darling!

My darling Renata, today is your birthday and my thoughts and heart are with you. Right at this moment I would love to see your smiling eyes, hear the whisper of your voice, and feel the touch of your hands. Today, however, I can only wish and dream. I have to be patient and trust my belief that at some point this moment will come.

June 4th - Tuesday

This morning, just before the arrival of Signore Vastola, we got into a heated discussion with the Albanians. Luckily, it ended without a fight. Idbed has tried and partially succeeded in replacing Henryk with one of his own countrymen. He pressured and negotiated with Signor Vastola to fire Henry for not showing up for work last Saturday and Idbed's buddy was hired in his place. From that moment on, the Albanians outnumbered me three-to-one.

June 6th - Thursday

Today was the 13th and my last day of work for Signore Vastola. These past two weeks were very good for me. Besides the excellent working conditions, I earned a few bucks and I practiced my Italian. Another advantage is that time passes quickly when you are working: around camp, time drags. In addition, I learned some basic farming skills. All in all, it was an interesting experience and I am glad I did it, but I realized that it's definitely not my 'cup of tea.' My future career lies in the electrical field.

Dziennik Polski, the Polish newspaper published in England, announced that UEFA, during a meeting in Switzerland, decided to ban all English football clubs from international competitions for a non-specified period of time. This is supposed to give the English soccer authorities time to get a grip on the hooligans, who presently dominate football stadiums across England.

June 8th - Saturday

Dear Renata: Thank you darling! Today I received a package from you, which Mrs. Irene sent from Rome. What a shame that I couldn't meet up with her during her short visit to the city. I found out about her arrival after receiving this package and by that time, she had returned to Gdańsk. Reading Krystian's words brings tears to my eyes. I know I should be stronger, but it is very hard not to think of the three of us, and the times we could be sharing together. From time to time, I allow

Krystian in May of 1985

my imagination to drift away from this cold, filthy place to our warm, clean, cozy home. There I can imagine our beautiful boy peacefully and innocently sleeping; he looks like an angel. His eyes are closed and his tiny lips are open. We can hear him breathing and now and again as he smiles in his sleep. He must be dreaming. During the daytime we build castles out of wooden blocks. Every once in a while you come to check on us and then quietly disappear to continue your daily household activities. Even though these thoughts are unrealistic today they fuel my faith in a better future for all of us. I'm glad that in the next few days you'll be going away for a holiday to Kołobrzeg with Krystian and my Mom. You really need this short get-away. Hopefully the weather is going to be as good as we have here in Italy.

Piazza del Popolo, Latina, with 'handsome' (L) and 'waiter' (R).

This morning, Mirek Kostrzyński-or 'handsome,' as some of us call him-has permanently left the camp. After 78 long days, he was transferred to the Fogliano Hotel, which is a small hotel on the beach seven kilometres away from Latina. He is the first of our gang to move out.

June 11ᵗʰ - Tuesday

More than two weeks ago, the communist authorities in Poland started a court trial against the three leaders of the Solidarity Trade Union: Michnik, Frasyniuk and Lis. The trial is taking place in my hometown, Gdańsk, the birthplace of Solidarity, the first non-government an independent organization in the entire Soviet bloc. It all started in late June of 1980, when the Politburo (Central Committee) of the communist party in Warsaw announced a major increase in meat prices of up to 60%. This also included so-called meat products available in canteens at the Polish factories. The Polish workers reacted immediately and on the following day, strikes broke out in Warsaw factories and then quickly spread to the south-eastern city of Lublin. These events consequently sparked waves of strikes in northern Poland, particularly at the Lenin Shipyard in Gdańsk. After more than two weeks of strikes, on September 3rd, the communist government signed the August Agreement, also known as the Gdańsk Agreement, ratifying all 21 of the workers' demands, including the right to strike. Sixteen months later, Solidarity and all other democratic organizations were banned and their leaders detained overnight. The following morning, thousands of soldiers in military vehicles patrolled the streets of every major city in Poland. The communist government declared Martial Law. A curfew was imposed, all national borders were sealed, airports were closed, and road access to all major cities was restricted. Telephone lines were disconnected, mail was subject to censorship, classes in schools and universities were suspended, and all independent communist government organizations, including Solidarity Trade Unions, were outlawed.

International news correspondents were prohibited from entering the courtroom and there were only a few permits issued for family members. The communist officials assigned a pro-government judge, Krzysztof Zieniuk, to oversee the trial and, together with state prosecutor Muszyński, they represent the regime. All three defendants were accused of, and charged, for their leading roles in the anti-communist organization known as the Temporary Coordinating Committee and for disturbing the public peace by promoting and organizing the 15-minute strike on February 28, 1985. The accused were represented by a strong team of advocates such as Anna Bogucka-Skowrońska, Grzegorz Jerzy Karziewicz, Tadeusz Kilian, Romana Orlikowska-Wrońska, and Jacek Taylor. During Friday's hearing, defendant Michnik was thrown out of court for the third time. Judge Zieniuk, with his 'Soviet-style' trial methods, does not tolerate any resistance or comments from either defendants or advocates. The trial is expected to end in the next few days.

June 13th - Thursday

After 83 days, Jurek 'vet' Majewski left this rotten hole and moved to the Caty Hotel, a small hotel on the coast of the Tyrrhenian Sea. At the Caty Hotel the food is better, the rooms are cleaner and have warm water, and overall the living conditions are more civilized. Jurek wants to immigrate to

Catching some sun with 'vet' (R)

Montreal where his father has been living for a number of years. He is the second person in our gang to leave the camp.

In Gdańsk the trial circus continues. This past Monday, a leader of the banned Solidarity Trade Union, Lech Wałesa, was called to the stand as a witness. He arrived at the court wearing a t-shirt bearing the Solidarity logo.

June 15th - Saturday

I can't believe it! First Mirek, then Jurek, and now Wojtek, the 'waiter' . . . In a nutshell, I am the only one left of our four-person gang who met in the transit area nearly three months ago. From now on, Wojtek will live in the Barba Hotel in the suburbs of Rome. The hotel's location isn't great – it's far from the city centre – but the good food and clean rooms compensate for the commuting challenge. On top of this, the hotel is equipped with a pool and a tennis court. After Wojtek's departure I inherited his black and white TV. Finally our room is properly furnished. Even though the TV is over ten years old, we don't really care. Now we have access to seven channels, all in Italian of course.

This evening was quite interesting. The street next to the camp was decorated in bright and glittering neon lights and wooden kiosks. The local vendors were selling toys, souvenirs, and freshly prepared kebabs. The smell of food was so good and it looked so delicious that I was very tempted to break the L100,000 note that I was carrying in my pocket. My conscience, however, kept my hands away from it. After all, I don't have a job.

Around 9 p.m., the procession headed towards the nearby Roman Catholic Church. This religious convoy of people was following a tractor bearing a magnificent statue of Saint Anthony surrounded by beautifully dressed little girls. On reaching the church square, the procession stopped and the skies lit up with a spectacular fireworks display. The festival lasted until late into the night.

June 17th - Monday

I spent the last two days in the Sporting Residence, which was full of refugees. I went to visit Leszek, who moved there nearly a month and a half ago. The majority of residents complain mainly about the food, which apparently is worse than in the camp. In addition, the hotel owners frequently turn off the power, sometimes for up to 12 consecutive hours, which leaves everyone without music, radio, or television. People are frustrated and a few times went on strike, but nothing changed. However, I haven't come here to check on the living conditions: I am here to visit the Polish Consulate. At around 9 p.m., both Leszek and I enter the iron gates of the Consulate. I have to admit it is not easy for me. I feel insecure. Here I am back on communist soil, but this time voluntarily. After 40 minutes of waiting, Mr. Józef Orewczuk invites me into his office. The quick handshake, suspicious-looking eyes, and the intimidating tone of his voice remind me again that I'm on communist soil . . .

What are you still doing here?
Where do you live?
What is the purpose of your stay?

I am bombarded with these and many more questions. Even though I feel pretty uncomfortable, I am extremely calm. Here again my creativity is very helpful.

"I'm inviting my wife and son for a short holiday to Rome. Afterwards, all three of us are planning to go back home (Gdańsk) where I want to open a boutique store with my mother."

Honestly, I have no idea where this story came from, but it definitely has to have impressed the commissioner, Orewczuk. He congratulates me and hopes my business prospers in Poland. Before I leave his office Mr. Orewczuk signs the handwritten letter of invitation, which should help Renata to get a passport and eventually join me in Italy.

JACEK LASZKIEWICZ   Krym, 1985.06.14
ul. POMORSKA   94A/64
80-333   GDAŃSK
PD NR.   294162

upoważnienie

Ja Jacek Laszkiewicz, urodzony 05.01.1963 r.
w Gdańsku, zamieszkały w Gdańsku ul. Pomorska 94A/64
posiadający paszport seria PD NR. 294162 wydany przez
WUSW w Gdańsku. Obecnie od 17 marca 1985 czasowo
przebywam we Włoszech. Wyrażam zgodę mojej żonie
Renacie Laszkiewicz, córce Ryszarda z domu Niedźwiedzka
urodzonej 02.06.1963 w Gdańsku, zamieszkałej w Gdańsku
z dzieckiem Krystianem Laszkiewicz urodzonym 14.02.1983
w Gdańsku.

Obecnie zamieszkuję u kuzyna żony
   Bruno Pietraccali
   via Francesco Baracca 19
   Montenero Di Bisaccia.
Przyjazd żony wraz z dzieckiem podyktowany jest
chęcią spędzenia wspólnych wakacji we Włoszech
w okresie 02.08 do 30.08.1985.

                                               Jacek Laszkiewicz

Ambasada P.R.L. w Rzymie
Wydział Konsularny

Nr 5040/178/85
Stwierdzam własnoręczność podpisu
.... Laszkiewicz Jacek
zamieszkałego w Gdańsku
.... Banp. PD 294162
legitymującego się
Krym., dnia 14.06. 1985

                              Kierownik Wydziału Konsularnego
                                   Józef Drewczuk
                                   Radca Ambasady

Letter of invitation signed by the Polish Consulate in Rome.

June 19th - Wednesday

Today, both Wiesiek and Mirek had their first and only interview for Australia. A Consulate interviewer told Wiesiek that he would need to find private sponsorship to be allowed to immigrate to Aussie land. Mirek, on the other hand, came out of the room soaked through and mentally exhausted. The interviewer focused on his political motives for wanting to immigrate and on his underground activity in communist Poland. He was asked a multitude of questions. In less than a month he'll find out if he's been accepted. Today I also received my fourth letter from you, Mom!

June 21st - Friday

On June 14, 1985, the court trial in Gdańsk ended. As everyone expected, all three suspects were found guilty in this government-staged trial. Michnik was sentenced to three and half years, Frasyniuk to three, and Lis to two years. This verdict initiated waves of protests across Poland and abroad. John Paul II, along with the American, French and other European governments, expressed their dissatisfaction with the Polish justice system controlled by the communist regime.

Later this afternoon I find out that Małgosia, Adam, Artur, and Mariola, and her son passed their interview and they are all welcome to immigrate to the United States of America. Darn, they're so lucky . . . Congratulations to you all!

June 23rd - Sunday

Tonight, around midnight, a tragic event took place in Building B, also known as the 'family building.' Two Albanians, armed with knives, attacked a Polish immigrant in the hallway and stabbed him three times in the stomach. Thirty minutes later, he was lying on an operating table at a local hospital. The operation lasted around two hours, and at that stage it was too early to say if he would survive. No one knew the reason for the attack, but it did not come as a surprise. There is a lack of trust and many cultural differences between the two nationalities.

Many conflicts are job- or theft-related. Generally Albanians speak Italian, which gives them an advantage in securing jobs and in securing the trust of the camp police. As a result, this leads to the mistreatment of Polish immigrants by the camp authorities. Of course, the exceptions are single Polish women, but that's a story of its own.

June 25th - Tuesday

Early afternoon, I go to the hospital to visit Zdzisław Michalak, the victim of Sunday's stabbing. My visit is short and last only ten minutes. He is sharing an eight-person room. Lying in the centre of the bed with an intravenous drip attached to his arm and a urine pouch underneath his hospital bed, he looked weak. Zdzisiek, a 25-year-old bearded, slim man, is planning to immigrate to Canada where his brother lives. Apparently he was stabbed with a pair of scissors, not a knife, and both his liver and a kidney were slightly punctured, but there is no immediate danger to his life. He looks tired and his speech is slow.

"Do you remember the attackers?" I ask.
"I do. One of them had stitches on the knuckles of both his hands."

I leave the hospital, filled with disbelief and anger.

June 27th - Thursday

In February 1945, a few months before Germany and Japan capitulated, the *Big Three* met in Yalta to discuss the future of Europe and its new borders: The Prime Minister of Britain, Winston Churchill; the President of the United States, Franklin Roosevelt; and the Russian leader, Joseph Stalin. The three reached an agreement on a new outlook for the European continent, governing a post-war Germany and Poland's domination by the Soviet Union. When the Second World War ended, the Soviet-imposed communist government was established in Poland. Most Poles felt betrayed by their wartime allies.

Eleven years later, on June 28, 1956, one of the first labour uprisings against Soviet-controlled Poland took place. In the early hours of the morning, the workers started a spontaneous strike at Cegielski's factories in Poznań. They demanded better working conditions, more pay, and were protesting a recent increase in taxes and higher work quotas. The workers took to the streets, and were soon joined by workers from other factories, students, and intellectuals, resulting in over 100,000 people gathering in front of the Imperial Castle, which is surrounded by buildings occupied by the party authorities and the Civic Militia Headquarters.

A peaceful demonstration soon turned violent as crowds took over a prison, freeing political prisoners and seizing firearms. Demonstrators attacked the Communist Party Headquarters and the secret militia building. In response, the communist authorities mobilized 10,000 soldiers and ordered in tanks, armoured vehicles, and field guns. Nearly 60 civilians were killed, hundreds sustained injuries, and over 700 were detained until August. Nonetheless, the Poznań protests were an important milestone on the way to the installation of a reduced Soviet—controlled government.

June 29ᵗʰ - Saturday

ONE HUNDRED DAYS . . . !

Yup, exactly 100 days ago I arrived in Latina. This unusual anniversary passed with no special fanfare or celebration. Only Wiesiek and I are left in this rotten place. All the other 'gang members' have left the camp and live comfortably in their clean hotel rooms.

Early this morning, nearly 200 refugees left for Rome in the hope of getting hired as extras in some World War II Italian production. Two headhunters representing the *De Paoli Studios* were in search of nazi-like individuals. After

In front of the main gate.

hours of waiting in a line-up, I was rejected. I guess I won't have a chance to wear a nazi uniform after all. In the next two weeks we should find out who was selected. Apparently the new extras are expected to get paid L60,000 per day. Not bad at all.

July 1st - Monday

Yesterday, I went to the hospital to visit Zdzisiek. He's looking much better than last week. He is in stable condition and quickly recovering. Since Friday, Zdzisiek is off his IV and yesterday he tried his first hospital meal. He had started to write a letter to his wife who lives in Poland with his three children.

Zdzisiek told me that after my Tuesday visit, three police officers visited him. They showed him photographs of possible attackers, to see which one he recognized. Apparently the attacker was arrested later on and is now in police custody.

July 3rd - Wednesday

There is a new system for distributing food in the camp. Instead of having separate lunches and dinners, both are now combined. This new system comes with pros and cons. One of the main benefits is the fact that we don't have to line up later in the afternoon to get food. The main disadvantage is that our meal portions have gotten smaller. Dinner doesn't come with warm soup or potatoes any more. Also, since both meals are distributed at the same time, the line ups are horrendously long and we can wait up to one hour. But the biggest concern is that when we are out working all day, we miss out on both meals and have to buy supper for ourselves and that can become very expensive.

Today Zdzisiek was discharged from hospital. After Father Andrzej's intervention, Zdzisiek has been moved to the Barba Hotel to prevent any further attacks on him. He only spent 11 days in hospital and I can not understand why such a short time. However, I found out that if the victim of an attack stays longer than 15 days, he might be entitled to compensation. I guess that would make sense.

July 6th - Saturday

Late this morning, 144 refugees were transferred to the Milo, Claudia and Residence Sporting hotels. Heniek, with whom I shared the room, was transferred to the Sporting Hotel in Rome after spending 106 days in the camp.

It takes nearly a whole day on a train to get from Gdańsk to Nowy Sącz in southern Poland. The state-owned railroad system, or PKP, is generally inefficient, outdated, and never on time. However, we arrived to our destination early afternoon, slight delayed, with the remainder of a day to spare. This is my second or third training/boot camp since I started judo. There are 25 or 30 of us representing our club. After the room assignment in a local elementary school building, our home for the next two weeks, six of us ran out to the school grounds to simply check around. Here we found that the school neighbours have a fairly sizeable private garden full of apple and plum trees, and some veggies too. It didn't take long for us to call for an 'invasion.' One after another we climbed over the fence to fill up our hungry stomachs and empty pockets. We're like the vultures feeding off of road kill on the Botswana roads or the raccoons penetrating the rubbish leftovers in the Canadian back alleys. After the long minutes of this fulfilling invasion we heard the angry voice closing up on us: "You sons of bitches, I will kill you all." Like grasshoppers, we jumped over the fence and quickly ran back to the school. We stopped gasping for air, saying, "Oh man that was close," and then we burst out laughing. This, however, was far from over. The owner of the garden snitched on us to our coach who immediately called for an emergency meeting. We are all lined up in the hallway of the school. "WHO, and I repeat WHO EVER was stealing from the garden next to the school, step forward." Then he added, "If no one will admit to this crime the whole team will be penalized." It took us about two minutes to step forward. Each of us was asked to get down on our stomachs on the cement floor. Then the coach used the wooden stick to whip each of our behinds six times. It was painful and embarrassing but taught us the lesson to stay on the right side of the fence in the future. The rest of the evening we were inspecting our bruised cheeks, laughing again.

July 8th - Monday

This past Saturday and Sunday night, camp riots took place between Poles and Albanians. The tension had been growing since Friday, when one of the Romanians viciously beat up three Poles with a wooden table leg. Rumour has it that he was a former wrestling champion – but this is not confirmed. The tension reached its peak when five Albanians armed with metal batons and wooden sticks attacked Bogdan, a Polish seaman. That was it: Riots broke out, and dozens of Poles and Albanians started to fight. Consequently, three police vehicles arrived at the camp, armed with black batons and pistols. The police started to search the rooms and forcibly removed their occupants. Their attitude towards the Polish refugees was aggressive and filled with hatred. The Police search started in our building. They were looking for any kind of weapons like sticks, knives, etc. They used force to enter each room, kicking down the door or breaking the locks or the door hinges, and they beat up a few residents.

Our room was no exception. Tomek Szkopiński from Wrocław was punched by one of the police and was arrested. He had arrived at the camp just a month beforehand. Tomek, a taxi driver by trade, had joined us in the room shortly after Heniek's departure to the Sporting Hotel. This came to be pretty unfortunate for him. The Police escorted him and many others to their cars and left the camp. However, camp riots continued despite this quick intervention by the police.

Around 1:30 a.m., Albanians again provoked the few Poles in Block G by throwing bricks. Ten minutes later, the police were back, but this time reinforced with *carabinieri*, the National Guard. Wiesiek and I were watching the whole event through a small gap in our open window, with the lights off so as not to draw attention to our room. We could hear people screaming as they were violently beaten by the *carabinieri*. The attack this time was much more brutal than before. A few minutes later the mass arrests of block G tenants started. At least 50 people had been taken away to the local police station. Some were aggressively hit with black batons while they were being loaded onto the trucks. The whole police action took no more than 40 minutes. Immediately after this happened, the Albanians looted the empty rooms. One of the immigrants went to report this to a camp guard who ignored him and said, "It is impossible. All the Albanians have been arrested." The guard warned him to go back to his room or he would also be in trouble.

The remainder of the night was peaceful. Next morning Father Andrzej went to the police station to discuss the previous night's events. The police officials showed him the confiscated weapons and told him that 66 people had been arrested, all of whom would be charged and would appear in front of a judge. Later on, around 12:30 p.m., we had a meeting with the church officials. During the meeting we underlined the fact that the local police and Albanians are well connected. The church asked us to write a report on the previous night's events and submit it to the local court.

Tonight, 28 people were released from police custody in two groups, among them Tomek. The night he was arrested he ended up at the police station at around 10 p.m., where each suspect went through detailed screening and then selected beating. Four were placed in cells with alcoholics, and then joined by another six, then 20, and then around 3 a.m. the remainder arrived. All were transferred to a local jail. Each person went through what was called the *'Path of Health,'* which was commonplace in the Eastern Bloc prison system. The armed prison guards would stand in two rows, creating a narrow pathway through which prisoners had to run while being hit by the guards. Those who the guards pushed to the floor or who fell of their own accord usually ended up with serious cuts and bruises.

Afterwards, all those arrested were thrown into cells occupied by local convicts. Tomek ended up in a cell with a so-called 'Papa' who had been sentenced to seven years for armed assault. Other inmates were serving sentences of up to five years each.

The cell itself was very clean, with a morning newspaper, and a black and white television set. Each jail mate is equipped with a propane bottle and a burner for independent cooking, an espresso machine, and a petty cash account for day-to-day spending. At 5 p.m. on the Sunday, Tomek, handcuffed, went to the court for the trial or hearing, which lasted no longer than an hour and half. The judge warned each of them that the next time they are arrested, they will be deported back to Poland. I wonder if he was bluffing or if he had the authority to do that. After the trial, all were loaded onto a police truck, taken back to the police station, and later released.

July 10th - Wednesday

Since the camp riots, the local police are on standby and officers check the rooms on a regular basis to make sure everything is in order. Also, a new system was implemented in the kitchen: Anybody who is trying to by-pass the line-up is sent back to the beginning of the line. What's really amazing is the complete change of attitude towards the Poles. The staff members are now very friendly to us: But are they being sincere? I guess we'll find out soon.

July 12th - Friday

I am working again, although it's not a permanent position. It never is. Punctually at 4 p.m., an old red Opel picks me up and four hours later I am back in camp. I'm getting paid L8,000 so I can't complain, and the job is fairly easy, weeding around tomato plants. Tomorrow is a day off.

July 14ᵗʰ - Sunday

Yesterday, from early afternoon on, Wiesiek and I watched 'Live Aid' from Wembley, England, and Philadelphia in the USA. This megashow lasted until the early hours of this morning. The fundraiser was dedicated to the starving people of Ethiopia and the rest of the African continent. Stars like Phil Collins, Mike Jagger, Bob Dylan, Tina Turner, Paul McCartney, Elton John, Jimmy Page, Robert Plant, Queen, the Cars, Police, and Tears for Fears performed and each band was on stage for around 20 minutes. In both Wembley and Philadelphia, there were huge screens for those watching farther away from the stage. Apparently a few stars boarded a plane immediately after finishing at Wembley to go to Philadelphia to continue their show. There were also concerts in Australia, Austria, West Germany, and Yugoslavia.

July 17ᵗʰ - Wednesday

Thirty-eight lucky refugees left for Canada today. This starts my record keeping of all immigrants heading to the land of great opportunities.

Also, since the beginning of this month, I have received the six letters from you, my love. Forgive me that I mention receiving these letters with such delay but there were too many things happening in the camp. I promise to stay on top of the things from now on.

July 19ᵗʰ - Friday

Today Jurek Majewski, the 'vet,' had his first interview for Canada. As Jurek's father has been living in Montreal for the last 20 years and is sponsoring his son, nobody really got excited. The one thing that did surprise us, however, was the fact that Jurek was a 'no-show' at the Consulate. This reinforces the rumour that he has gone back to Poland. Apparently, Polish authorities have refused to give his wife and children passports. Is this the only reason for his return?

July 22ⁿᵈ - Monday

Today more news. First, Adam and Małgosia are leaving this coming Wednesday for the United States. Adam came from the Barba Hotel to tell me the news. They are heading to Los Angeles, California, where Adam's family is apparently waiting for them. En

Małgosia, Adam and me (L) at Lido di Ostia in Rome.

route, however, they are stopping over in New York where they will spend one night. Then they fly to Chicago, and after a two-hour layover they will finally arrive in LA, the host of the 1984 Summer Olympics. Adam invites me for a beer and a few hours later, I accompany him to the train station where we finally go our separate ways. The train leaves at 6:15 p.m.

Wiesiek also received good news from an organization in Melbourne that is helping him with the immigration process. If he's lucky, he will be spending Christmas in Australia . . .

Today, another flight left for Canada, this time with 25 people on board.

July 25ᵗʰ - Thursday

Yesterday, a Canadian delegation led by John Holm visited the camp. The camp officials organized a meeting with the Consulate representatives and the refugees who are either waiting or applying for immigration to Canada. I was there, of course. The meeting was quite informal and one point was stressed: The lucky ones who go to Canada will be treated as Canadian citizens, not as immigrants. John Holm also added that on arrival in Canada we will be allocated private accommodation and will be sent to school to study English. However, we won't be helped in searching for jobs. In the first year, we will receive a grant to live on. There's no information on how much it will be, but it sounds good anyway. Education is free up until the age of eighteen and after three years of living in Canada we'll be able to apply for Canadian citizenship and eventually a passport. During the meeting, one of the Polish immigrants asked the consulate an interesting question: "How many immigrants is Canada planning to accept by the end of this year?" Mr. Holm's answer was vague: "Around the same number as last year."

Right after the meeting, I went up to Mr. Holm and asked him when I could expect my first interview. "September or October," he replied. "Fantastic – only two or three months to go," I say to myself.

Yesterday, the Italian authorities questioned me about political asylum. The odds of getting asylum are very minimal. One in a hundred gets it.

July 27th - Saturday

This past Wednesday, the kitchen went back to the old system of distributing individual meals, as a result of an anonymous vote among the refugees.

Today, I received my fifth letter from you, Mom. With the letter, you enclosed a Polish newspaper cutting referring to the riots in Latina. The title of the article was 'Bloody Riots in Latina' by Ambrożewicz. The article is quite biased and it looked like the journalist didn't bother to investigate the true reasons behind the riots. I'm quite sure Ambrożewicz became well known after his article was released to the public.

My parents divorced when I was six or seven years old. It was hard emotionally and financially on my Mom. For a year or so we lived on Konopnicka Street in a bachelor suit in Gdańsk Wrzeszcz (the Gdańsk district). Later on we moved on Pomorska Street where my Mom still lives in the very same one bedroom apartment we moved into during the early '70s. It was tough, but somewhat manageable. I guess as a single mother she didn't have too many options. Nearly every month when she was getting paid she used to take me out to the Mocca Café in our neighbourhood where she ordered a lemon tea with a slice of cake for me and a black coffee for herself. Routinely she would light a cigarette in enjoyment. Strangers would approach her, commenting how well mannered this little boy was at the table. This made her smile proudly.

July 29th - Monday

Another flight to Canada, this time with 35 refugees from Poland, each of whom had been waiting an average of eight months.

July 31st - Wednesday

The last day of the month is pretty lucky for us. Wiesiek Staśko and I have an opportunity to make some extra cash. Simon, 27, picks us up at the camp in his FIAT Ritmo and we end up on a farm picking green beans. During this eight-hour day, a 73-year old 'Grandpa' supervises us. I have to admit Grandpa can outwork all of us: This guy is unbelievable. His stamina and farming skills were impossible to beat. Around 10 a.m., we have a breakfast of Kaiser buns with baloney and lots of water. Punctually at 2 p.m., we finish work and each of us receives L25,000. We are working tomorrow as well and have a wake-up call at 5:15 a.m.

August 2nd - Friday

Yesterday, I didn't make it to work. I felt pretty crappy and hadn't slept practically the whole night and so I asked Heniek to cover for me. He had come back to the camp nearly a month ago because he couldn't find work in Rome. Now, he sleeps, eats, and works wherever and whenever he can.

For 63 days the underground resistance fought the Nazi aggressors in the sewers and cellars. Tens of thousands of civilians were slaughtered week after week, the city districts reduced to rubble as the Red Army watched from across the Vistula River. The 1944 Warsaw Rising was a pivotal moment in the outcome of the Second World War and the division of Europe between the western coalition forces and the Soviets.

Sadly, nobody in Latina recognized today's anniversary.

August 4ᵗʰ - Sunday

After three exhausting days of work, today was a well-deserved day of rest. Heniek has joined our three-person team and we are picking Roma plum-style tomatoes on a farm. The work itself is not hard but the heat (36 C) is really getting to us. Our productivity is nowhere near expected; after all, we are city boys not farmers. The farm is located in the foothills of a small city known as Seeze, 20 kilometres south of Latina. The size of the tomato field is about three hectares. It looks like we are going to spend a few more days here, which is not bad at all.

August 6ᵗʰ - Tuesday

It's been five days since I started to work for Simon. Today, after eight hours of work, we managed to get Grandpa talking. He seems to have a good sense of humour and is willing to learn a few Polish phrases. I'm guessing that Grandpa is in his seventies and he's an extremely well-skilled farmer. None of us can keep up with him picking tomatoes. Today we sent the first 6,000 kilogram load to a depot. We estimate he'll get paid around L140 per kilo, which adds up to about L800,000 per load. Not bad, considering that we are expected to send five more loads.

August 7th - Wednesday

Wiesiek decided to sign up for the United States rather than endlessly wait for Australia. Most likely his decision has been influenced by the fact that his own uncle, who has been living in Australia for nearly 40 years, was not interested in helping him with the immigration process. Wiesiek has wasted five long months, which must be really frustrating.

Piazza della Liberta, Latina, with Wiesiek (C) and 'kid' (R).

August 10th - Saturday

The last four days gave us fantastic cloudy weather. The gray skies bring relief and shelter from this dreadful heat and fill us with renewed energy. We are ready to conquer the fields. As a result, two more loads of this red fruit will end up at the depot. On the way back to Latina, Simon stops at the depot. I've never seen anything like it: endless line-ups of trailers, trucks, vehicles filled with Roma tomatoes, waiting to dispose of their lucrative loads. It can take up to 20 long hours to sell one load. Wow!

Wojtek Kowalczyk left Italy today for the United States after waiting 141 days for this moment. Of the guys I met in the transit area when I arrived, he is the first to leave.

August 13th - Tuesday

Another two days of work behind us. The weather is still good, the heat wave is over, and the temperature is more manageable for working. Throughout the entire day of *lavoro,* we sing and whistle, which animates Grandpa to the point that he starts to whistle with us. We also learn that Simon is his son. After a long day on the farm, Simon invites all of us for a cold beer – which brings a smile to our faces – and we get to meet his two beautiful daughters, one aged two years and the other, six months. Besides his involvement on the farm, Simon is also building a house that he hopes to move into early next year. I take on the challenge of trying to explain to him why so many Poles are escaping from Poland. Of course my Italian skills are very limited, but by using my hands I am able to get the message across. It's funny how creative we can be when the situation requires.

August 15th - Thursday

Information, the continuous flow of reliable information, is really important for us in the camp. It doesn't matter if it arrives on time or not, as long as it arrives. Both good and bad news is absorbed and read over and over again. Good news strengthens us, bad news we try to forget. Whatever the news is, we are waiting for it, seeking it out.

Yesterday, I received two letters from you, numbers 16 and 17, with four pictures. Thank you my love . . . Kocham Cię, "I love you."

August 17th - Saturday

The 13th, and last, day of work. Today there are only two of us, Wiesiek Staśko and me. Grandpa doesn't join us, but that doesn't stop us from working hard and efficiently. At around 2 p.m., Simon arrives to take us back to camp. He is very pleased with our work and mentions the possibility of more work in the next few days, perhaps on the 26th.

August 20th - Tuesday

Finally . . . ! After three days of deliberation, Wiesiek S. invested in a new camera. The new toy is a 36mm frame Olympus OM-10 and cost him L367,000, or US $200. Before he made this major purchase, both of us had spent long hours studying photo magazines and catalogues. The only limiting factor was budget. Wiesiek seems happy and relieved after this investment. For now I can only share his joy and wait for the day when I'll be able to dispose of my ancient Russian SLR and get something more respectable, like a Japanese Nikon or a French Leica.

August 21st - Wednesday

Today was the second time Jurek Majewski's name was listed for a Canadian interview and, again, he missed it. This reinforces our theory that he is back in Poland with his wife.

August 22nd - Thursday

It has been five months (154 days) since Wiesiek Kowalski and I entered the gates of the camp. Both of us started this unknown journey together. Tomorrow marks the start of our sixth month here. In celebration, I secured a job. Oh crap, not again! POMODORE, POMODORE . . . tomatoes again! This time it's piecework: for every 15 kilograms of picked tomatoes I get paid L500. In nine and a half hours the three of us managed to fill 122 boxes and make L70,000 between us.

August 28th - Wednesday

Yesterday afternoon, I ran into Krzysiek, who works as a translator for W.C.C., (which takes care of my immigration process to Canada). Apparently, my file was sent to the Canadian embassy on August 13th, which is very good news. Now, it shouldn't take more than two months before my first interview. Hopefully I'm right about this.

I also received two letters (17, 17a) from you, my love. Thank you!

August 30th - Friday

Today, Krzysiek ('uczeń' – the 'student'), Weretka, arrived. He's from Gdańsk as well. The 'student' is a good friend of Adam and Małgosia and before Adam left for Los Angeles, he asked me to help him on arrival. Today's visit was short and lasted no more than 20 minutes. We shook hands, chatted for a while, and then the 'student' left for Rome to finish the tour he is part of. He should be back in Latina on the 6th or 7th of next month.

September 1st - Sunday

It is late at night and for the last couple of days *RAJUNO*, the Italian TV station, broadcast an extensive coverage of the fifth anniversary of the Solidarity Trade Union in Poland. *Telegiornale* (the evening news), showed the highlights from the demonstrations in Warsaw and Lech Wałesa honouring the shipyard workers who were killed by the communist authorities in 1970. He laid flowers in the shipyard. The leader of the banned Solidarity party wore a white t-shirt saying 'iron man' in French, in red. Also, Pope John Paul II mentioned this anniversary in his sermon in the Vatican. Unfortunately there was nothing organized to celebrate this event in camp.

September 4th - Wednesday

"Wczoraj po długich cierpieniach zmarł przeżywszy 20 lat nasz kolega uchodźca. Msza św. za duszę zmarłego odbędzie się dzisiaj 04.09 w kościele San Marco przy placu San Marco w Latinie o godz. 15.30. pogrzeb odbędzie sie na cmentarzu w Latinie."

"Yesterday after a long time suffering our 20-year old colleague passed away. Prayers for his soul will be held on September 4th at 3:30 p.m. in San Marco church. He will be buried in the Latina cemetery."

This shocking news was posted early in the morning on the bulletin board. We have been told that Zenek died of liver cancer, but this is unconfirmed. There were over 250 people attending the funeral service, half of these were Italians. Around 5 p.m., Zenek's coffin was laid in an earlier-prepared grave. Rest in Peace.

September 7th - Saturday

Me and the newcomer 'student' (R).

This past Thursday, the 'student' came back to Latina, this time for good. Without wasting any time we started all the required formalities. Krzysiek received an ID with the number 13371. Since my arrival five months earlier, he is the 2088th refugee registered in Latina. Like me the 'student' had also decided to apply for immigration to Canada. I warned him that he could wait up to one year before realizing his dream, but it didn't seem to worry him and he is prepared to wait. The first night he slept in my room; the following day, I found him accommodation across the hallway in room 54.

Yesterday I received letter number 11, which had been delayed for six weeks.

September 9th - Monday

Ninety-nine refugees left for Rome to a new hotel, Hotel Flaminus. There are rumours that this group is one of many expected to leave Latina in the near future. Fortunately my name wasn't on the list, I am staying in camp . . .

September 11th - Wednesday

Exactly three years ago, we vowed to love and be faithful to each other. I remember, it was a beautiful sunny Saturday. I would never have imagined that three years later, on our wedding anniversary, we'd be apart from each other. On that day everything seemed so simple. We had each other, and were happy and deeply in love. However, the reality of starting a family in communist Poland was harsh; we didn't have our own place to live in and we were not willing to wait up to 30 years for a state-owned apartment. This is when both of us reached this decision, which is crucial for our future. Today I am confident that it was the right decision and I don't regret it at all. I know that every day that we are apart strengthens my feelings for you. Today my wish for us is to be patient and to love each other. I hope that our journey together will be filled with mutual trust, respect and love.

September 13th - Friday

We are flooded with news from the Residence Sporting Hotel, where Polish refugees went on strike demanding better food. From what I understand, Czech refugees did not join the Poles.

There's a new name list on the bulletin board, this time including 69 refugees. Destination: Hotel Flaminus. Departing tomorrow. I'm still unsuccessful; I'm staying in the camp. A few of those from the list will return to the camp later on to look for work as it's very difficult to get any work while in the hotel. They will rely on us to give them accommodation and sometimes even food. Many will sleep on the cement floor, and only a few will be lucky enough to find a bed.

September 17th - Tuesday

Six months away from home. Exactly half a year ago, I left Gdańsk in search of a better tomorrow. The time I have spent here in Italy didn't really add anything significant to my life except improve my personal survival skills. These may be useful at a later stage in the future. For now, I live from day to day, struggling to get work and studying English, usually by myself. Neither this language nor my day-to-day life comes easily.

On this unusual anniversary, I am fortunate enough to get work. The 'student' (Krzysiek), the 'kid' (Jacek), my new mates, and the 'taxi driver' (Tomek) are also lucky. All four of us end up in a vineyard picking grapes. In eight hours we harvest approximately five tons of the fruit. The work is not bad and in fact it's fairly easy compared with picking tomatoes. Our new boss is pretty happy at the end of the day and he pays each of us L40,000. This is my new daily payroll record, which up until now was L30,000.

September 20th - Friday

In less than seven days, on September 27th to be exact, I have to go to Rome to the Canadian Consulate on Via Zara for my first interview. The day beforehand I need to go to the C.I.M. to pick up my train ticket. The interview list includes 23 names. This is the second list posted in the last two weeks, which makes us believe that Canada has finally started to accept immigrants. This is the same situation with the United States and Australia.

September 22nd - Sunday

News from America! I received the first letter from Małgosia and Adam. They have been living in the States for the last two months. Adam found a job in some manufacturing company while Małgosia is still looking for work, possibly as a draftsperson. Of course they brag about their first major purchase, a car, for which they paid US $ 975. The next step is to buy a flat. Małgosia adds that communication between the Poles in California is very minimal or even poor. I'm sad to hear it, but not surprised. When I lived in Poland, I heard about the lack of unity between Poles in exile. At that time, however, I was so far away that it didn't really bother me. Or so I thought.

September 24ᵗʰ - Tuesday

Thirty-one refugees left for Canada yesterday. The next flight is expected next month.

September 26ᵗʰ - Thursday

This afternoon, Tomek Szkopiński had his first and only interview for the United States. He is pretty positive about the outcome. He was hoping to be accepted and be on a plane to America within a month. Today is his last day in camp as he and many others are on the list to leave for the Claudia Hotel, the same hotel that Wiesiek Staśko left for on Friday. This will be the fifth group to leave. In all, nearly 300 refugees have left the camp, and another 300 arrived.

September 28ᵗʰ - Saturday

Yesterday, along with eight others, I had my long-awaited interview for Canada. I got up early and after shaving, I brushed my teeth, quickly dressed and left for the train station. After less than an hour the train stopped at the Termini station in Rome where Wiesiek Staśko was waiting for me. We arrived at the Canadian Consulate a few minutes before 9 a.m. It took nearly an hour before I was invited to the Consul's office, and I was fourth in line. For the first 15 minutes I was questioned about my education and work experience in Poland, and for the last ten minutes the Consul told me what I could expect on arrival in Canada. During the interview, I had to sign a few papers which are required for immigration. One of the key conditions of immigrating to Canada was an agreement to immigrate to Manitoba. At the end of the interview, I asked the Consul a few questions regarding reuniting with my family, and I was happy with his answer. He told me I could expect the second interview sometime in January or February next year. However, before that, I will be called for a medical exam.

October 2nd - Tuesday

A few hours ago unexpected news hit the camp. Apparently Jurek Majewski, rumoured to be back in Poland, has returned to Latina with his wife and child. It seems like all the gossip about his return to Poland is not true. Apparently two months ago, Jurek had crossed the border into Austria where his wife and child were waiting for him. The three of them then crossed the Trieste checkpoint to come back to Italy. Now, they continue their immigration process as a family and are waiting for Canada.

October 5th - Saturday

In the last few days, nothing sensational happened in this immigration shoebox. In the first three days of October, I made some extra money, L100.000 to be exact. Although the work was quite hard and strenuous with no food, it was at least manageable. I can't really complain though: After all, I'm an illegal worker here and there are ten others ready to take on my position. Also, I prefer a full rather than an empty wallet as it gives me a sense of security, independence, and overall it makes me feel better – psychologically more balanced.

October 7ᵗʰ - Monday

TWO HUNDRED DAYS IN CAMP.

Has anything changed in the camp since my arrival in March? Generally speaking . . . no! The washrooms, the hallways, and the rooms are still filthy and disgusting. However, a few things have been done to improve our living conditions. Of course there is a slim chance that the walls will be painted or there will be hot water in the bathrooms. The roof, however, is continually going through structural repairs. The toilet stalls now have doors, which is a huge bonus as we can now squat with our pants around our ankles without being seen. Meals? No major changes here. We are still running on a week-to-week menu

Preparing scrambled eggs.

and it doesn't look like this will ever change. After only two weeks of arriving, we already know which meal will be served on Thursday or Saturday. Some people like the predictability; others don't. However, rather than complaining, we should be happy to have food on our plates.

As far as we know, the Albanian problem has almost gone away. The camp authorities now recognize that the easiest way to control any unrest between Albanians and Poles is to minimize the numbers of each nationality in the same camp. The only way to accomplish this is to scatter both nationalities between different hotels. The Polish school has re-opened its doors after closing last summer. Unfortunately, due to the limited number of teachers available, the program has been restricted to a few subjects only. The English lessons have returned to the curriculum as well. They seem to be quite popular at the beginning and then gradually the number of students decreases, and only a few will finish the whole program. There is still a lack of cultural activities in the camp. Nobody seems to be interested or have enough skills to take the lead. Most of us are immersed in our own problems and challenges. We arrive, we leave – at some point we will leave – and then newcomers will repeat this process over and over and over again. The camp in Latina is educating and forcing us to survive, and to trust only in ourselves.

October 9th - Wednesday

Three years ago, in 1981, the Solidarity Union was banned by the communist regime. Even though the whole nation and 12 brave senators voted against the decision, that wasn't enough for the communist dictatorship government in Poland. Solidarity has been outlawed. Yesterday's anniversary was turned into a day of national grief and was mourned by thousands across the country and beyond.

October 11th - Friday

For the last three days, I have finally been working in my profession as an electrician. Jacek Binek 'kid', the newcomer to Latina, joined me. He has no clue or any electrical background, but that has no real relevance when finding work. We all learn our skills on the job. The 'kid' now shares the room with us – we brought him in after the 'taxi driver,' Tomek, left for the Claudia Hotel.

Today is the first day of an outdoor market. This will last until on Sunday night. This event attracts thousands of shoppers and people who simply love browsing around. At the fair you can find and buy nearly anything, from a little bracelet or a window frame to even a camper.

Our work is to supply electricity to each stand, kiosk, or booth. There are approximately 100 stands to be hooked up and we run approximately five kilometres of cables. It's a tough job, but after ten hours of work we get paid L90,000—not a gold mine, but better than nothing. After the few months of living in Italy, I've learned one thing for sure: Pride is good, as long as it does not affect my wallet.

Some letters were censored.

October 13th - Sunday

Last night, I went to a local cinema to watch *Missing in Action*, an American action-movie set in communist Vietnam. Colonel James Braddock (Chuck Norris) is a retired US army officer who spent seven years in a North Vietnamese prisoner of war (POW) camp, and then escaped ten years ago. Now he returns to Vietnam in search of American soldiers who were listed as 'missing in action' during the Vietnam War. He and his old buddy, Tuck, launched a mission deep into the jungle to free American POWs from General Trau. Considering the low budget of Joseph Zito's movie, the clip was pretty intense and good. The film was played in the same cinema in which, each Tuesday, x-rated movies are shown.

October 16th - Wednesday

Fifty-two refugees left for Canada – mainly Poles. I only knew one of them: Krzysiek used to work as a translator for the organization that is taking care of my immigration process. He and his wife left after 11 months and one day.

October 18th - Friday

Dear Renata, a few minutes ago, I finished reading the 28th letter from you. It upsets me to hear that you are continually struggling and fighting with your Dad. I cannot believe he treats you that way. You are the mother of our son and he has no right to shove you around like this. I was planning to write him a quick note, but after thinking it over I decided not to . . . I don't think it would be much use sharing my anger on paper. I am disappointed that your Dad is not respecting your hard work and how much effort you put into raising our Krystian. You can count on me for words of encouragement, love, and friendship.

October 20th - Sunday

The Solidarity supporters demonstrating in Rome.

One year ago, on October 19, 1984, Polish secret police brutally murdered a Roman Catholic priest and an anticommunist activist, Jerzy Popiełuszko. He and his driver, Waldemar Chrostowski, were kidnapped. The priest was beaten and stuffed in a sack weighed down with stones and thrown into the Vistula River. His driver managed to escape and spread the news about the priest's abduction. Popiełuszko's body was found two weeks later on October 30th. In memory of this tragedy, a memorial service was held at the church on Via Botteghe Oscure in Rome. Nearly 300 people attended, mainly from Latina. After the service we walked through the streets of Rome to Capitoline Hill where, on the stairs leading to the church of Santa Maria in Aracoeli, we laid flowers in a cross formation and lit candles.

This peaceful demonstration attracted the attention of bystanders. This was the first Solidarity-organized demonstration outside of Poland that I participated in.

October 23rd - Wednesday

Tonight the 'kid' (Jacek Binek) left for Germany; it took him only three months. On his last night, we had a few drinks and a little feast: slices of bread with lard, chopped onion, and cheese. Oh gosh, is this ever so good! Tomorrow afternoon he'll arrive at his destination, Germany.

October 28th - Monday

Twenty eight left for Canada today. The next flight is expected early November. In addition, 150 refugees have been transferred to a camp near Capua, in southern Italy. Albanians and Vietnamese are mainly occupying Capua; there are a few Poles as well, but they are mainly waiting for Canada and Australia. Apparently the living conditions and the food are much better than here in Latina. The main disadvantage is the long distance from Rome, an additional 200 kilometres. Also, it is much harder to find work there. Władek and Zdzisiek Nowak are in Capua, both of whom are privately sponsored for Canada.

November 1st - Friday

All Saints Day (the Day of the Dead) - is traditionally a day of mourning and reminiscing about those who have departed to eternity. This evening, we visit graves to light candles and place flowers for those of whom we have fond memories and those who are unknown to us. The atmosphere is unique and by night the cemeteries are decorated in the glowing and flickering lights of thousands of candles, many in colourful glass jars.

November 3 - Sunday

For the first time in my life, I am picking olives. There are six of us: three Romanians, Zdzisiek Nowak, Krzysiek Romanowski and me.

Krzysiek arrived in Latina from Toronto in Canada where he worked illegally for ten months.

Today's weather was awful, with torrential rain and howling winds. Harvesting olives is fairly easy, but after two hours it becomes boring and monotonous. We worked only three hours and we will continue tomorrow, weather depending, of course.

November 6 - Wednesday

Today is my long-awaited medical exam. Up until this morning, I was pretty anxious and was wondering if they would ever call me for this exam. For the last two weeks, I kept checking the bulletin board for my name. My anxiety and doubts over whether I passed the first interview kept growing until this morning's list was posted on the board.

"Buongiorno," I said while stepping into the small room . . .

"Good morning," the doctor replied. After a few general questions he asked me,

"What is your weight and height?" "Darn! What the hell is my weight and height? 175cm? 64 kilograms?" I ask myself.

After a thorough examination the doctor looks up at me and, while holding my right hand, he asks, "Did you ever have two thumbs on this hand?" "Yes, I did," I respond, and add. "The second one was amputated when I was two years old." This conversation is followed by an x-ray and blood tests. Assuming I pass these, I will obtain clearance for the second interview, which most likely will happen early January.

November 8th - Friday

This is our fourth day of picking olives. For the last three days, we have had fantastic sunny weather. The temperature during the day reaches 20 C, which is way better than in Gdansk at this time of the year. None of us are really keen to work too hard. Each morning, the Italian gives us a hard time for the previous day's productivity, but we're not worried and we continue to work at our own pace. The 'spaghetti head' has paid us L25,000, which is not bad considering that finding work at this time of year is tough.

November 11th - Monday

Independence Day!

"One century and a half of battles, sometimes bloody in casualties, triumphed today. One century and a half of dreams of a free Poland finally came true today. Today we are celebrating a big day, the day of happiness after a long night of suffering. On this hour, in a heartbeat I have the honour to open this senate, home to all of us."

With these words Josef Piłsudski opened the first Parliament in 1918 in independent Poland. Less than 30 years later, these words became obsolete with the Nazis occupying Poland between 1939 - 1945.

November 12th - Tuesday

Today, on your Name Day, I would like to give you a bouquet of blue forget-me-nots. This flower is close to my heart and reflects my feelings for you. Its purity and gentleness remind me of you: its fragrance reminds me of your body; the petals remind me of your hair covering your bare shoulders; and the baby blue colour reminds me of your heart, which I miss here. These few words are insufficient to express my feelings for you, but they come from the depth of my loving heart.

November 14th - Thursday

Another departure for Canada. This time the list includes 38 names. This might be the last flight of the year. The next flight is expected sometime in January.

November 16th - Saturday

This morning, I participated in a rat chase. The chase took place in the washrooms, and then with the speed of a rat, moved to the hallways. We won: The rat is dead! This was one of many hunts in the camp, but the first one for me. Victory is claimed.

November 22nd - Friday

Killing time.

It has been pouring with rain for more than a week now. Needless to say, we are all grounded in our rooms. There is nothing to do except play cards, write letters, and watch the hands of the clock slowly moving. I am becoming quite good at cards: out of fourteen games I won eight and this ranks me number one. The 'student' has won six games. Wiesiek and Krzysiek are in our shadows. Oh well, some win, others lose.

At 2:30 p.m., both Wiesiek and I start our ninth month in Latina.

November 26th - Tuesday

Two hundred and fifty days on Via XXIV Maggio 3. Have the camp authorities really recognized this unusual anniversary or is it simply fluke that today they decided to transfer both of us to Rome? Who knows? But it doesn't really matter.

Hotel World is in the city suburbs and entirely occupied by refugees. The hotel complex is made up of two neighbouring buildings. I imagine this generates respectable revenue for its owners. We, the refugees, guarantee a cash flow.

We are both assigned to the same room, number 104. Immediately after opening the door to our new nest, our excitement was short lived. In hotel terms this is supposed to be a two-person, fully-equipped suite, but it now accommodates six people. There are two pieces of furniture remaining from the original suite arrangement, consisting of an old chair and a small cabinet. Both pieces are used as tables. There are three existing tenants: Marek (recently transferred from Istanbul refugee camp) and Artur are both from Poland, and Victor Smigalski, the oldest guy, with a good sense of humour, is from Romania. Victor speaks a little Russian so we are able to communicate to some extent. Our sleeping arrangement is a bunk bed. After a short and heated discussion, we agreed that I would take the top. The only really good outcome of today is the fact that now we have our own bathroom and it is much cleaner than in the camp. Apparently, every few days the rooms are cleaned as well. The cockroaches and other living creatures are now part of my distant past. I won't hear or feel them crawling on me tonight. The day ended with quite a decent meal and a hot shower. Not bad at all. Goodnight!

November 27th - Wednesday

Right after lunch I packed my personal things and went back to Latina, arriving at the camp before dinner. The reason for my unofficial return is to make some extra money before Christmas, which was around the corner, and to pick up my mail.

November 29th - Friday

This afternoon I secured three hours of work and was paid L15,000, not bad for a short day of work. What was unusual about this job was that the work was arranged the day before, which rarely happens in Latina. A middle-aged fellow spotted me on the sidewalk and hired me to work with him in the Enel warehouse, loading concrete utility hydro poles onto a truck, and then, later on, offloading them at another location. In total we did six of these trips. Ricardo was in charge of the crane. My work was limited to securing the area while loading the poles on the truck. It was fairly easy and a manageable day.

Today letters 35, 36 and 37 arrived. Thank you, Hon.

December 1ˢᵗ - Sunday

Urszula, Krzysiek's wife who lives in Poland, has been in Rome since Thursday. I worked with Krzysiek last month picking olives. She came to Rome to see him after the long, one-year separation. She arrived in Rome as part of a group of 30 and is scheduled to be here for one week, and then she's expected to go back to Poland where their two-year-old son, Adam, waits for her. The group is staying at the Daniela hostel, near Termini train station. There are two separate buildings with a common reception area. Urszula's room is located away from the monitored area, which allows Krzysiek to spend a few nights with her. Lucky him!

This morning, I met them both in Rome to start our sightseeing trip around this magnificent city. I am their unpaid personal photographer for the day, equipped with a Zenit 11, my Russian state-of-the-art camera. Actually though, this is not completely true: I am getting paid . . . with sandwiches and pop, etc.

Our journey starts at Piazza Venezia in central Rome, next to the gigantic monument of Vittorio Emanuele II, the first King of the united Italy. In 1885, Giuseppe Sacconi designed this enormous white marble monument, today often referred to as the 'wedding cake' or 'typewriter' due to its shape. Next, we take Via Del Corso to the nearby 18ᵗʰ century Fontana di Trevi. This impressive fountain dominates the small Trevi Square located in the Quirinale district. In 1732, Pope Clement XII commissioned Nicola Salvi to design and build this large fountain. Construction was completed 30 years later, in 1762. Tradition holds that tossing a coin into the fountain guarantees your return to Rome. Nearly L10,000,000 are collected here daily. This inspires Krzysiek and Urszula to throw their change into the fountain and it's a good time to get out my camera and take a few shots of my happy clients.

Our next stop is Capitoline Hill, the smallest of the city's seven hills. Each day thousands of tourists visit the Piazza del Campidoglio, which is on top of the hill. The current appearance of the square, which was designed by Michelangelo, dates back to the 15th century. Three buildings surround the square: Palazzo Senatorio, Palazzo dei Conservatori, and Palazzo Nuovo. During Roman times it was the religious centre of Rome but now it is more of a historical one. It is home to the Capitoline museums and its famous bronze sculpture of a She-Wolf suckling twin infants, Romulus and Remus, the founders of Rome.

Here we stop for a short break. Krzysiek's attempt to find an original Italian pizzeria ends up in a fiasco and we end up having *Peroni* (Italian beer) and sandwiches for lunch instead. I don't mind—I never refuse a free lunch. Our last stop is the most recognized landmark of Rome: the Colosseum. There are hundreds of books, travel guides, plays, television programs, films, photographs, and of course stories about this incredible architectural phenomenon; as far I'm concerned, adding more to this pot of common knowledge will not benefit anyone. We are here, standing on Via dei Fori Imperiali, looking at this elliptical amphitheatre, with Piazza Venezia behind us.

"Move to the left. Little bit more. Smile." Then snap, another photo taken. Before I catch the train to Latina we stop at the hotel to have supper. Urszula lays out on the table some Polish sausage and a bottle of *Żytnia* (grain vodka), neither of which Krzysiek nor I have any problems finishing. My train leaves Termini station at 8:15 p.m. It was a good and eventful day.

December 6th - Friday

Today's numbers: 832 refugees in camp and 2,639 scattered between the hotels in Rome, Capua, and suburbs of Latina. These are the official numbers released by the camp authorities. Yesterday Urszula left Rome and went back to Warsaw, loaded with Christmas gifts.

December 12ᵗʰ - Thursday

Hooray . . . more money! Krzysiek, Zbyszek, Wojtek, and I do some work at a small construction site. We end up working for the whole morning carrying 60-kilogram cement bags and floor tiles up to the fourth floor. In other words, 'MEN AT WORK.' During a short break we get some cookies and a beer. After a few minutes, we're back at work again. For the next two hours we hoist buckets of sand to the third floor, which is much easier than carrying bags of cement. We return back to the camp around noon. Zbyszek, an electronic engineer working with me, is physically shattered, his body aching from exhaustion.

December 14ᵗʰ - Saturday

Wow . . . what a surprise! Yesterday I received a Christmas parcel from you. You can't imagine what a huge surprise it was! I was really stunned by all the gifts you sent. Of course the photo album and the framed photos are fantastic, and as soon as I get back to Rome I will hang them above my bed. Now, next to our little Krystian, you will be my guardian angel. Every morning I will touch your lips to say "Good morning, my love." In the evening, I will send you a kiss goodnight. As you wished, I will light four candles at our Christmas Eve dinner. The necklace is beautiful and I will wear it that night. Thank you, my love, for such a beautiful gift representing your feelings and love to me. ILY!

It is obvious, the ZOMO militia units do not have any fear of the protestors throwing stones, bricks or carrying the anti-communist banners and shouting anti-government slogans. The ZOMO and the SB (secret service agents) are more concerned with the protestors armed with the 35 mm cameras and their darkrooms at home. The developed photos are far more powerful than broken windshields on the ZOMO vehicles. The photographs always find a way of reaching the hands of news-hungry American, German, or French journalists where they will eventually get published in the Times, Le Figaro, or Der Spiegel magazines. This typically ignites waves of demonstrations across the streets of Western Europe or America and puts pressure on the governments of the Eastern Bloc.

Just like in the past, I decided to take my trusty 35 mm Zenit with me. It takes guts to raise both your hands to point and shoot under these circumstances. You had better be a safe distance away or be prepared to run fast in case you are spotted by any secret service agents or militiamen. If you are captured, you will lose your camera. And if you're lucky enough, you may end up with only a few bruises on your back. The ZOMO militiamen are well known for their brutality and are well paid for this purpose. The masses are supposed to fear them, and the majority does.

Before I had time to realize what was happening, two uniformed militiamen dragged me into a van with four or five other protestors. The first rule, when you are arrested, is to stay calm and not to share too much of your personal information with others. There could be a snitch among the captured. You just never know. We arrived at the militia station one hour later, around 6 p.m. After hours of intimidation, questioning, and threats, I was released. It was 1:30 a.m. I maintained possession of my camera, but all my negatives were confiscated by the ZOMO interrogators. I am pissed off, but happy to be free.

December 18th - Wednesday

After three months, the 'student' leaves the camp for the Barba Hotel. This news made a few people happy as he was not well liked by his roommates. To be honest, he is not easy to be around and in the last short while he has annoyed me as well. Today, one day before his departure, I decided to go back to Rome. I'll be back in Latina on Tuesday, though. One of the main reasons I keep returning here is obviously work opportunities, which are so limited in Rome.

December 21st - Saturday

Marek and I are excited about this morning. We are going to visit Villa Borghese, a huge public park in Rome, and at the last minute Artur decides to join us. It's a little chilly but in less than two hours the sun will come up and it should be another beautiful day in Rome.

Cardinal Sciplione Borghese established Villa Borghese in the 17th century. The park is dominated by the magnificent palace, which became home to the finest works of art by the great Italian Masters dating back to the 17th and 18th centuries. Unfortunately, we cannot afford the ticket to get in. We keep on moving slowly towards the lake where, during the summer time, you can rent a small boat. At least now it's winter and that's not an option. Our savings are in our pockets. There is a small island in the middle of the lake, and the lazy floating birds disturb the still surface of the water. Nearby, an elderly man is sitting on the rusty bench catching a few morning rays of sunlight. Further along, under the shade of a tree, a young couple is sharing their love. Villa Borghese is an oasis of peace and rest. Many locals come here after a long day of work to catch a breath of fresh air and enjoy the serenity and isolation. In the northern part of the park, on Aldrovandi Street, is the zoo. The tickets are L3000 each, which is about $1 per person. Hmmm . . . after a few minutes of thinking it over, the decision is NO.

It's now time for *colazione* (breakfast), and after finding a bench, Artur opens his pack for the long-awaited bottle of champagne and some pastries with raisins. Hallelujah . . . What a fantastic treat! We'll take the bus on the way back to the hotel.

Another load of people has left for Canada, this time a group of 19.

December 24-26th CHRISTMAS

This year, Christmas will be completely different from any other in the past, far away from home and family. Christmas in Gdańsk is always cold and the days are short; in Italy, the days are warm and sunny. Two weeks before Christmas, the sidewalks of Rome and Latina are covered with bright red carpets and Christmas trees that are temporarily placed in planters. The shop windows are beautifully decorated and look inviting. Christmas Eve is one of the most celebrated days of the year, both in Italy and in Poland. The majority of shops and department stores are open for extended hours. Shopping, however, is quickly tapering off with the passing hours. It's not the best time to shop, as prices are at their highest and last-minute shoppers pay a premium. The big sales, however, will start shortly after the New Year celebrations.

This year's Christmas is not only different, but it will also be remembered for many years to come. I started my day early in the morning. After a quick breakfast, I went upstairs to my room to dress: grey trousers, v-neck sweater, dress shirt, and a navy tie. Today we have another gathering with Pope John Paul II, this time at the Paul VI Auditorium in the Vatican. This is the third time I am going to see

Historical meeting in the Vatican
March 18, 1985

him in person. The first two times I saw him were back in March when I was still touring Rome, and on the very first time I saw him, I attended a private audience with him. At that time, I got to shake his hand and say a few words to him. It was strange but at that moment I felt unexpectedly calm. There were pictures taken and greetings were exchanged but I cannot recall exactly what his Excellency told me.

Wiesiek, Marek and I arrive at St Peter's Square before 10 a.m., still two hours to go before the audience with the Pope will begin. In one hour, the Polizia and the Swiss Guards will open the auditorium, which will quickly fill up with 6,000 pilgrims from all over the world singing and laughing. I see a few familiar faces among them. Przemyk and I used to share a room in Latina. "Wow . . . he looks bad . . . and he's still in Latina," I think to myself. I guess his drug dealings are now keeping him in Italy. I also run into Bożena, who is waiting for her flight. And then I see Tomek, who now lives in the Hotel Claudia near the city centre. Three months have passed since his interview for the United States. He already has sponsorship but for some reason, he's still in Italy. At around 11 a.m., 20 buses full of refugees from Latina and Capua arrive at the square. It looks like the Vatican is paying for it all. Later on, I spot the tallest person in the crowd, which is Wojtek of course. Who else is here? I scan the crowd to find Zbyszek and Krzysiek.

Half an hour before noon, the 9,000-capacity auditorium is half full of worshippers and pilgrims alike. In addition to the large contingent of Polish immigrants, there are pilgrims from Poland, and TV and radio correspondents, and, of course, newspaper journalists. At 11:50 a.m. Pope John Paul II is entering the auditorium, welcomed by thousands. The standing ovation never stops; people are smiling, and shouting Pope John Paul II's name. He smiles, greets the pilgrims, and for the next 60 minutes he shares his wisdom with us. At the end he walks along the barriers to shake hands with people. It is amazing that four years ago there was an attempt to kill the Pope but this doesn't seem to stop him interacting with the crowd. Arturo Mari, an official photographer for *L'Observatore Romano* (the Vatican newspaper), is busy taking hundreds of pictures, which later on will be on sale in the Vatican store. I am standing next to the barrier holding my Russian Zenit camera, and in the next few minutes I will touch the Pope again. "Please, let us in," I hear behind me. A young mother with her new three-week-old baby is trying to get John Paul II to bless her baby, Marek. The Pope stops and blesses the newborn. I feel tears running down my cheeks. It's a very emotional moment. Wow. What a day! And it's not even halfway through.

Christmas Eve dinner with Krzysiek (L) and Wojtek (C).

I am now on the bus heading to the camp for Christmas Eve. During the commute between Rome and Latina we talk about the audience with the Pope and tonight's supper. Before we sit down at the table, there is a heap of work to be done as no one has prepared anything. I stop by Standa, a local department store where I spend L10,000. Oh crap, it is already 5 p.m. and we are nowhere near ready. There is no way we'll eat borscht or have the carp ready for this Christmas Eve: There is not enough time. Krzysiek and Wojtek are struggling with a potato salad, Zbyszek is on a mission to find a hot plate, while I am cleaning the room and getting the table ready. Finally, around 8 p.m. we are ready. We shake hands, kiss each other on the cheek and then, following our tradition, break the Christmas wafer and hand it to one another with a blessing – just like back home. Next we sit at the table and eat. First tuna and then, after our main dish, the potato salad . . . Oh my, it is so good. Krzysiek did a fantastic job. Fruits and sweets will come later for dessert.

My love, I wish I could be with you now. I can only guess how empty this evening is without me at the table. Do not worry, because soon we'll be together again. My heart is with you both. Can you hear the whisper of my voice? I am wishing you the very best. We sing carols 'lulajże Jezuniu, moja perełko . . .' in the candlelight. We are together in mind if not in body: not even distance can separate us. Our love and faith will win and soon we will be reunited.

Exactly at midnight, we all head to the church to attend Midnight Mass, where we pray, sing carols, and then take communion. I feel spiritually connected with everyone around me and the atmosphere is fantastic. Next day, I wake up with a big headache. Gee, I think I have a hangover. For the whole day, I eat only biscuits and vegetables and drink mint tea.

December 29th - Sunday

This morning's highlight is our trip to the Vatican City to explore the Musei Vaticani. Marek, Wojtek, and I leave the hotel early in the morning. The museums date back to the 16th century, built for Pope Julius II's personal sculpture collection. Since we are short of time, we only tour sections C and D. We start in the Egyptian sections with the nine rooms full of sculptures, monuments, statues, and artifacts. Then we move to the Belvedere Palace, followed by the Upper Galleries and Raphael's Rooms, with the Battle of Vienna, a masterpiece by Jan

Matejko. This magnificent victory over Kara Mustafa's Turkish army was led and won by the King of Poland, Jan Sobieski III, who is referred to as the 'Saviour of Vienna and Western European civilization,' Another good reason to be proud of our Polish heritage! The Sistine Chapel is our last stop – the location of the Papal conclaves and Michelangelo's masterpiece. I'm disappointed and I have no idea why. Perhaps it's the overwhelming crowd filling the chapel? One thing is for sure: I'll be back here again. On the way out we walk through the Sistine Hall of the Vatican library, one of the oldest libraries in the world. It is very impressive.

Exhausted, we head back to the hotel, and now I can feel how tired I am.

December 31ˢᵗ - Tuesday

On the last day of 1985, I decided to write a letter to Mr. Hetman Director of Grupa Studiów Emigracji Polskiej in Osna, France. It reads:

Roma, 31.12.1985

Dear Mr. Hetman

On October 8ᵗʰ this year I sent to the G.S.D.E.P. the second and last part of my journal entitled 'Latina 1985.' To this day, I haven't received any confirmation from you or your staff that you received it. There are others here in a similar situation. The deadline passed exactly two months ago and we still don't know the result of this competition. I neither know nor understand the reason for this silence. On behalf of other participants and me I would like to ask you to let us know immediately the results of this competition. You should also know that many participants have already left Latina and have immigrated or live in different locations in Italy. Let me thank you in advance for your positive response. My new address is;

Hotel World
Via Cliento, 3 – Roma – Tel. 898641
Telex 614063 – Sidero
Chiesetta Nel Parko

Regards
Jacek Laszkiewicz

There are only a few hours left until the New Year. Artur has organized and financed the food, snacks and booze. We prepare the supper together: sausages, canned meat, and pop – mainly Cola. After 8 p.m., Krzysiek, Zbyszek, and Wojtek arrive from Latina. They brought with them five bottles of cheap sparkling wine. For the next two hours we drink and talk. Around 10 p.m. we leave the hotel and head towards the di Trevi fountain in downtown Rome. Since public transit is very unreliable we walk there – it takes us nearly an hour.

Only 30 minutes left until midnight and the New Year, 1986. The international mix of partygoers arrives at di Trevi. We gather around Rome's famous landmark, along with Americans, English, Germans, French, and Italians. Exactly at midnight, fireworks, crackers,

Celebrating New Year's Eve at Trevi Fountain.

and a dense cloud of smoke fill the plaza. We open the first and then a few more bottles of 'champagne.' We shout, scream, and exchange good wishes. The atmosphere is fantastic and like a carnival. Some drunken guys dive into the freezing water of the fountain and you can see the camera flashes going off.

It is not over yet, though, and I have no idea what possessed me to do what I did next. Together with a complete stranger from England, I climb the statue of Neptune, which towers over the fountain. We are nearly 25 metres above the marble fountain, water, and cement. The

King of the Baltic Sea surrenders under our feet. We shout, laugh, and wave our hands to those below. A few minutes later, the police arrive, but too late: we made it down in time and safely headed away to the Spanish Plaza. Twenty minutes later we join the big party at the Spanish Stairs. This is one of the most beautiful and colourful parts of Rome, tonight occupied by drunks and party animals. Here we finish the remaining bottles, which we throw away, empty, on the stairs. They break into pieces and the *carabinieri* are not too happy with the shattered glass. The 20 or perhaps 30-metre distance separating us from the police gives us a false sense of security. Luckily we are able to prevent any arrests and around 2 a.m., soaked through and cold, we are on our way back to the hotel. I get to bed at around 6 a.m. and promptly fall asleep.

January 2, 1986 - Thursday

In less than a week I am scheduled to be at the Canadian Consulate for my second, and hopefully last, interview. This will be the most important meeting, and my immigration to Canada depends on it. There are five other names on the list for the same day.

January 4th - Saturday

Yesterday I received the 46th letter from you, my love.

January 5th - Sunday

Happy Birthday to me, I am 23 years old!

January 7th - Tuesday

As we planned earlier, Marek and I went to explore Aventine Hill. Once populated with the aristocratic society of Rome, today it is one of the city's most elegant suburbs. We mainly concentrate on the three churches: Saint Anzelmo, Sant Alex, and, the most beautiful, Santa Sabina, built in the fifth century by Peter of Llri. Here the Blessed Czesław and Saint Jacek, founders of the first Polish Dominican Order, started their missionary work. Santa Sabina is famous for its dark cypress-wood doors, carved with biblical scenes. We make our way through the doors to discover 24 stunning marble columns dividing the basilica into three naves. In the central nave, on the floor, we find the tombstone of Munoz de Zamora, a General of the Dominican Order. It is a very unique tombstone where the image of the dead is depicted as a mosaic. We are pretty amazed and culturally enriched. Next, we take a quick walk to the end of Via di Santa Sabina to the Piazza dei Cavalieri di Malta (Square of the Knights of Malta). The square itself is rather plain, but that is not the reason we are here. Marek and I join a queue in front of the wooden doors of the Villa of Malta. We cannot enter the premises but we can take a peek through the most famous keyhole in Rome. The view is extraordinary: The copper-green dome of Saint Peter's Basilica in the Vatican.

On the way back to the hotel, we stop at Santa Maria in Aracoeli, situated on top of Capitoline Hill. The church is famous for its wooden statue of the infant Jesus (Santo Bambino), carved in olive wood in the 15th century and revealed to the public once a year at Christmas time.

January 9th - Thursday

Well, that's it. My second interview is behind me. It lasted just six minutes, including a telephone call that the Consul received while I was in his office. The main difference between today's interview and my first interview is the lack of feedback from the Consul. Shit, I'm not too happy with this! Now I am pissed off as I am not sure if everything went okay or if I screwed something up. Now I have to wait to find out if I am accepted or not. There are 14 long days in front of me.

January 13th - Monday

Right after lunch the hotel owners force us to leave our room and move to another building in the hotel complex because of the arrival of a new family from Iran. Apparently, our room was too large for us after the departure of Victor and Boguś. Let's face it, we actually anticipated this would happen sooner rather than later. Both Marek and I started to move our belongings, while Wiesiek was still visiting Latina. Artur, on the other hand, is working in Rome. After two hours of slaving away we sit down to rest. Eighty-eight is our new room number, until now occupied by a mother with her son. The new room is much better than the last one and, in addition, we have a phone. We still share a common bathroom, but we have our own boiler, which guarantees us continuous hot water. A married couple and their two-year-old son occupy the room next door and they are also from Poland. We conclude that this move was definitely for the better.

January 15th - Wednesday

It has been 300 days since I arrived at the camp. I cannot believe I have been here for so long. Who would ever have guessed?

There is a scheduled flight to the United States today. Tomek Szkopiński, the 'taxi driver,' as well as 75 other refugees, will board the plane. In addition there was a flight to Canada this past Monday with 31 people on board from our hotel. The next batch is planned to leave January 30th.

January 20th - Monday

For the last few days, I have been writing letters home and also to my aunt and my cousin, Marek, who live in Germany. They left Poland in 1981, before martial law came into effect.

December 13, 1981, was a cold Sunday morning, our only day off from work and school in communist Poland. For many, Sunday starts with church and then a family breakfast; it is a day of rest and joy. I got up at around 10:30 a.m., and while I was getting something to drink in the kitchen, I overheard my Mom lamenting in her room, "Oh my God, the war has started!" "Mom, what are you talking about?" I asked, walking into her room. The First Programme of Polish Radio was on, the only radio station available this morning, announcing a state of martial law. I'm puzzled and I don't quite understand what that means. "This just doesn't make sense," I am thinking aloud. When we turn on the television at noon, we hear a familiar figure, General Wojciech Jaruzelski, representing the Military Council of National Salvation, announcing that martial law has been imposed across the whole of Poland. This is to 'defend socialism' against the extremist elements of Solidarność and other anti-socialist groups.

Without thinking twice I ran downstairs to the fifth floor with a winter jacket in my hand. I put on my jacket while ringing the doorbell on apartment 52. Tycjan and I head to Żabianka train station and 25 minutes later we arrive at the downtown Gdańsk Główny railway station. From here it is less than a ten-minute walk to Solidarity Square, which is opposite the entrance to the Gdańsk Shipyard. There are 6,000 workers behind the shipyard fence protesting the declaration of martial law. Armoured vehicles and tanks are outside of the Shipyard Gate No.2, with the gun muzzles pointing at the gate. The crowd is becoming larger around the Square. Many, including us, surround the tanks; a few place flowers in the gun muzzles, while others share cigarettes and even food with the soldiers.

Considering the circumstances of this terrifying morning, it's a strange scene. However, it is in keeping with our heritage: Poles are proud, respectful and acknowledge the role and importance of the military. We all stay calm and try to figure out what will happen next. It will be another three days (December 16th) before the tanks breach Gate No.2 and then the ZOMO begin the removal of the striking Shipyard workers. Over the next two days, the streets of Gdańsk remain a war zone. Continuous clashes with the ZOMO militia leave one civilian dead and hundreds wounded. Empty cardboard teargas containers are discarded on the sidewalks, streets, and rail tracks. The heavy cloud of teargas fills the streets, train station tunnels, and our eyes. It is challenging to keep our irritated eyes open without rubbing or scratching them. During this time, the ZOMO militia is also using water cannons and apparently rubber bullets. We escape to the train station platforms to hide behind the trains. We hear explosions and the hissing sound of falling teargas containers. One of them hits Tycjan in the ear, leaving him bleeding and in excruciating pain. We board the train with hundreds of others. Half an hour later a nurse will take care of Tycjan's ear. She won't record his name on the ER registry to protect him from any militia investigation or follow-up. Martial Law, communist's last stand, was lifted in 1983.

January 23rd - Thursday

Fountain of the Four Rivers at the Piazza Navona.

It is an early start today. Marek and I finish our breakfast around 7:30 a.m. and a few minutes past 8 a.m. we arrive at the Piazza Navona, the original site of the Stadio di Domiziano, used for athletic contests and for gladiator shows. Here, in the rays of the early morning sun, we continue the historical journey of Rome, the Eternal City. In the centre is the famous Fontana dei Quattro Fiumi (Fountain of the Four Rivers): the Nile, Ganges, Danube, and Rio de la Plata, representing the four continents. I take a few photos and now we head to Saint Andrea's church – dating back to the 16th century – built for Scottish expatriates. This church was frequently visited by the famous Pole, Adam Mickiewicz, a 19th century Romantic poet. Our next stop is the Pantheon – a temple to every known god of ancient Rome – built more than 2,000 years ago by Marcus Agrippa. Since the seventh century it has been used as a Roman Catholic Church. Michelangelo studied its impressive dome before he started work on the dome of Saint Peter's Basilica. Victor Emmanuel II and Umberto I, two kings of Italy, are buried here. I am completely captured and rendered speechless by both the simplicity and the complexity of this place, one of the oldest sanctuaries in the world. In my awestruck tour of the Pantheon I completely forget to use my camera and board the bus without any pictures of this magnificent site. We're back in the hotel before 1 p.m. in the afternoon, just in time for lunch.

January 26th - Sunday

I spent this morning in the Vatican Museum. This time I explore this magnificent place alone. Today, I am able to recognize an extensive collection of the Masters' works of art from centuries ago. I leave the Vatican sad, not knowing if I will ever come back here again. Back in the hotel room, my mind is replaying what I had explored a few hours earlier.

January 28th - Tuesday

To be honest, I just don't know how to summarize this day – or rather the first few hours of this morning. Shortly after breakfast, Marek and I left for the C.I.M. on Nomentana Street. As usual, there are long line-ups in front of the buildings. "When is my medical?" or "When is my interview?" or "When is my departure?" These are typical and ongoing questions asked by the refugees here. I am patiently, but nervously, waiting in line for my turn. After 20 minutes, I approach the unpleasant clerk, who sits behind the desk, to ask about my immigration status.

"I had my second interview for Canada three weeks ago but I don't know the result," I tell her in my broken English. It could be a minute or maybe even two, but it felt like hours waiting for her to find my name on the list. Finally, she slowly raised her head to announce, "You are going to Winnipeg on February 17th." I can hear her voice, but for some reason I can't absorb the content of this message. I am totally stunned. Here I am waiting for three weeks and suddenly this. I ask her again. "Can you repeat, please?" It is too late. Marek is already congratulating me. I still can't believe it. I have been waiting for this news for nearly one year.

January 31st - Friday

Enjoying the snowfall with Victor from Romania.

The past two days we had heavy snowfall in Rome. The whole city is covered with snow and is in a complete state of chaos: tire chains, fender benders, businesses shut down, and streets and sidewalks flooded. It doesn't look like Rome has any budget allocation for this type of eventuality. You can't really blame the city, as this only happens once every decade and then it becomes big news. After all, this part of the world is not known for heavy snowfalls.

February 4th - Tuesday

Today I received a reply from G.S.D.E.P. Director, Mr W Hetman:

> *Mr. Jacek Laszkiewicz*
> *Roma*
>
> *Dear Mr. Laszkiewicz*
> *I sincerely apologize that you neither received nor were informed of the results of this competition.*
>
> *First Prize   -   nickname 'Wilczyca'*
> *Second Prize -   nickname 'Przemysław'*
> *Third Prize   -   nickname 'KKS'*
>
> *The above winners will be published in the second quarter of 1986 in a bulletin. Your journal is very interesting and caught the attention of POW (a publisher). With your permission, I would like to ask you to give us the rights to publish parts or, if possible, the whole journal.*
>
> *Regards,*
> *W. Hetman*

February 8th - Saturday

I spent the past four days in the camp. I didn't really plan to stay that long, but there were still a few faces I knew in Latina and the 'goodbyes' lasted longer than I anticipated. It was actually quite pleasant visiting. The senior refugees ensure that their colleague is treated well during his visit to the camp. Everyone was inviting me to stay over, and I had no problem getting food; Zbyszek shared his soup with me, and either Krzysiek or Wojtek organized bread. I also collected my mail.

Lavoro? Work? Not a chance. There is a chronic lack of it. Via XXIV Maggio 3 is overloaded with refugees hoping to get work.

Buildings H and G have been renovated to some extent: new paint job, the ceilings have been repaired, and even the rooms have new doors. It looks much better now. Other than that, no major changes have been made. Bathrooms and restrooms are the same, dirty and smelly.

At 4 p.m., I am sitting comfortably on a train and ready to leave Latina for Rome. I take a last look at the station and the train starts slowly moving leaving behind the large blue sign with the white letters, LATINA. I bet that many people in the camp would love to be on this train today. I should scream and jump in the air with excitement; however, I am leaving Latina with mixed feelings. The train gains speed, leaving my

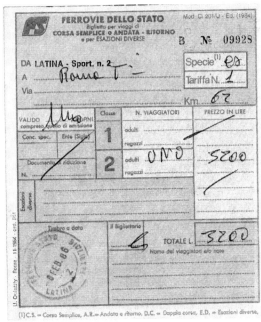

Train ticket to Rome.

memories behind. Now I think of all the things I have to do before my departure. These include laundry, packing, writing my last letters from here, and, naturally, having a few drinks with my buddies. I nearly missed my record keeping: There was another batch for Canada and this time there were 28 immigrants on the plane that left on January 30th.

February 9th-10th Sunday and Monday

Today I write and send my last letters from Italy. This closes the chapter of my correspondence here in Rome.

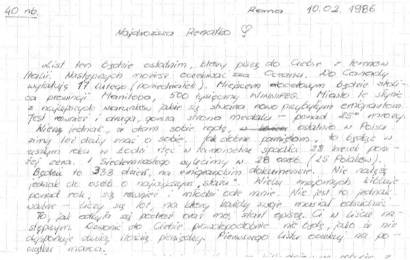

Fragment of my last letter to Renata from Italian soil.

February 11th - Tuesday

There are eight names on the list for Monday's flight, which has been posted on the bulletin board next to the hotel reception. My name is fifth on the list . . .

February 14th - Friday

Italia, Roma 14.02.86

Krystian, my dear son!

Today is your special day, your BIRTHDAY.
It has already been three years since your eyes captured the
loving smile of your parents.
I hope that this smile will accompany you into your
unknown future. Today I am sending you a greeting card
with a smiling bunny on it, and wish you happiness.
Even though we are apart, nobody can separate our
loving hearts.

Yours lovingly
Dad - Jacek

February 15th - Saturday

There are two more nights left until no more climbing up and down this darn bunk bed. Even though there is still a significant amount of time left, I am already packed and ready to go. I have only left a few essentials out that I will need: my toothbrush, toothpaste, soap, and clothes to change into. This afternoon we have a little party in our room.

February 16 - 17th, 1986 - Sunday, Monday

I haven't closed my eyes the entire night, my last night in Italy. No, not because I am nervous, but really because I was so worried about missing the early morning meeting at 4:30 a.m. in the hotel reception. My next night will be somewhere in Winnipeg, in central Canada. To occupy the slowly moving hours, we play cards, talk, and drink black coffee prepared and served by Wiesiek. We empty the fridge of any extra leftover food. After playing cards, we continue talking and laughing into the night.

"Kid, kid you are finally leaving!" Wiesiek says.

"Do you have warm boots, kid?" he continues, and then adds, "Kid, you will die over there on your own." We're all laughing.

"It is time to leave this shit hole. Just make sure no one pushes you around and don't worry about cooking, you'll learn quicker than you think," Wiesiek continues. I'm smiling and add, "I know how to brew tea and I can definitely handle scrambled eggs; it's my specialty." We're all laughing again.

Punctually, at 4:30 a.m., I am downstairs in reception with all my

Identification tag.

belongings – two packs. Artur decides to join me in the lobby. He stays with me until the bus arrives, which is really nice of him. Earlier, in the room, I had exchanged goodbyes with Wiesiek and Marek. The bus arrived a few minutes after 6 a.m., one hour late. All backpacks, bags, and suitcases are loaded onto the back seats. We are on our way to the airport now. The international airport, Leonardo de Vinci, is located in the suburbs of Rome, in a community known as Fiumicino. On the way to the airport, we pick up more people from Latina and Capua camps who had spent the night in the underground rooms of the train station in Rome.

Before 8 a.m. we arrive at the airport. There are 25 refugees in our group.

The flight is scheduled for 12:45 p.m. Now it is all about killing time, just like last night in the hotel. Some of us lie down on benches; some just walk around and browse the stores. Around 10 a.m. three bureaucrats bring our passports to us. This is the first time I have seen my passport in nearly a year. Now we all go through Customs – this will take right up until a few minutes before the plane is about to depart. Sixty immigrants will board the DC-10 today. Before we board, however, we invade the duty free shop where we buy Camel cigarettes and matches. I help another Pole to get a few postcards at the souvenir stand, after which we shake hands and walk in opposite directions. In the next few minutes, he will board a PLL-LOT Polish Airline plane. He is one of many Poles visiting Rome as a tourist. My travel companion is Mariola, also Polish, who is going to join her sister in Ottawa. I met her this morning in the hotel and she sits next to me in the plane. Flight number 203 leaves the gate with a 20-minute delay. We are all buckled up; smoking is not permitted. The good-looking stewardess explains the safety procedures and then takes her seat. The McDonnell Douglas DC-10 three-engine, wide-bodied Alitalia airliner safely takes off, leaving the memories of the past 333 days behind. I am airborne, on my way to Canada . . .

* * *

Four of us arrive in Winnipeg that night. Three of us are sponsored by the Canadian government, one by a relative. Two gentlemen representing the local government greet us at the airport, one of whom speaks broken Polish. A few minutes later we are all in the vehicle heading to downtown Winnipeg. The streets and sidewalks are totally white, and only the snow banks defined where the streets stopped and the sidewalks started. It is 25C below zero. "What the hell is wrong with this place?" I think.

After no more than 15 or 20 minutes, we arrive at our temporary destination, the Balmoral Motor Hotel on Cumberland Avenue and Balmoral Street, in the city centre. Heniek and I share a room for the

My first day in Canada.

next two weeks. Heniek is married, and his wife and three children are still in Poland. Wow, the hotel was luxurious after Latina! We had a colour TV, two comfortable queen-size beds, a fantastic buffet downstairs, and our own clean bathroom.

The following days we spend extensive hours at the government offices where all the formalities, including the rental of a bachelor apartment, are taken care of. At night we are totally absorbed, watching the National Hockey League in the hotel room TV. What a game – so fast! Edmonton Oilers with the 'magician on ice,' Wayne Gretzky, in action. During these first weeks in Winnipeg, each of us receives survival gear: parkas, winter boots, a dining room table, two chairs, a twin-size mattress, a set of cookware, and cutlery. In addition, we received a few bucks for public transport, food, and pocket money. Not bad, considering that I arrived here with only a backpack and US $10 in my pocket.

My first apartment is in a high-rise building on the sixth floor at 33 Haregrave Street in downtown Winnipeg. On June 2nd, three months after my arrival, I started my first job in Canada with an electrical manufacturer in the North Kildonan community of the city.

A year later I am finally reunited with Renata and Krystian, after two years, four months and four days . . . Krystian is nearly four and half years old, and is the most precious sight I have seen since I left Gdańsk.

EPILOGUE

Adam Domżalski	Returned to Gdańsk in Poland after living several years in California.
Artur Nieszczerzewicz	Returned to Warsaw in Poland after a living several years in Winnipeg, MB, Canada.
Henryk Lacheta	Lives in Edmonton, AB, Canada.
Jacek 'kid' Binek	Emigrated to Germany.
Jurek 'vet' Majewski	Rumoured to have emigrated to Montreal, QC, Canada.
Krzysiek Romanowski	Lives in Brampton, ON, Canada.
Krzysiek 'student' Weretka	Lives in Westminster, CA, USA.
Leszek Piłaszewicz	Lives in Edmonton, AB, Canada.
Małgorzata (Krynicka) Baumann	Emigrated to Switzerland after living several years in California.
Marian Skarzyński	Lives in Winnipeg, MB, Canada.
Mirek 'handsome' Kostrzyński	Returned to Warsaw in Poland after living several years in Australia.
Tomek Szkopiński;	Lives in Germantown, TN, USA.
Wiesiek Kowalski	Rumoured to have emigrated to USA.
Wiesiek Staśko	Rumoured to have emigrated to USA.
Wojtek 'waiter' Kowalczyk	Emigrated to USA.
Zdzisiek Nowak	Emigrated to Kitchener, ON, Canada.

ACKNOWLEDGMENTS

Over the past three years, I have had to overcome a number of hurdles to achieve my personal goal of writing this account. Thanks to the mutual efforts and unconditional support of a few people, these memoirs have successfully been published.

Katie, my wife and life partner has been an unfailing source of encouragement and support. My questions and sometimes desperate pleas for help have always been met with patience and a smile. Thank you, my love, for the many hours spent reading through the manuscript and for correcting my English!

I would like to thank my dear friends, Keith Inman and Anita Kuehnel, for all their valuable input and for editing the manuscript. I really appreciate your competence and your willingness to help me finalize this project.

And last, but not least, thank you to Brandon Jordan for his imagination and creativity in designing the cover for this book. Brandon has captured my journey from the darkness of those difficult times in the refugee camp to the hope, relief and, later, joy of my arrival in Canada.

My gratitude goes to you all!

CPSIA information can be obtained
at www.ICGtesting.com
Printed in the USA
LVOW12s0930050717
540322LV00001B/82/P